Praise for Joe Upton's *Journey through the Inside Passage:*

"Alternately exhilarating and contemplative . . . Upton's approach underscores the powerful effect of sea and land on those who choose to wrestle with them. These are realistic tales of adventure that can compete with the lure of television."

—*Booklist*

"Those who traverse Alaska's maritime world will find Upton exciting and authentic. . . . Armchair voyagers . . . will place the book high on the list of favorite maritime reading. *Journeys through the Inside Passage* is a winner."

—*Anchorage Daily News*

"Whether he writes of facing the rough waters of Queen Charlotte Sound alone or watching the sunset from an isolated settlement hacked out of the wilderness, Upton demonstrates on every page that he is a craftsman who knows how to reel in the right word and do it with no wasted effort."

—*Fairbanks News-Miner*

Other books by Joe Upton

Alaska Blues: A Fisherman's Journal
Amaretto

JOURNEYS THROUGH THE INSIDE PASSAGE

~~~

*Seafaring Adventures
along the Coast of British
Columbia and Alaska*

JOE UPTON

Alaska Northwest Books™
Anchorage • Seattle

Second printing 1992

Library of Congress Cataloging-in-Publication Data
Upton, Joe, 1946-
    Journeys through the inside passage: seafaring adventures along the coast of British Columbia and Alaska / by Joe Upton.
        p.m.
    Includes bibliographical references and index.
    ISBN 0-88240-366-4
    1. Inside Passage—History.   2. Inside Passage—Description and travel.
3. Seafaring life—Inside Passage—History.   I. Title.
F1089.I5U68 1992
917.95—dc20   91-28242
                                                                         CIP

All contemporary photographs are by the author. Historical photographs and illustrations are courtesy of the following collections:
    California Historical Society, San Francisco, CA: p. 164 (Photographer. W. E. Dassonville. FN-26339).
    The Jewish Historical Society of British Columbia, Vancouver, B.C.: p. 76 (Photographer: Leonard Frank. 24515).
    The Museum of History and Industry, Seattle, WA: pp. 22, 40, 108.
    Puget Sound Maritime Historical Society, Seattle, WA: pp. 11, 34, 169.
    Vancouver Public Library, Vancouver, B.C.: pp. 49 (Photo No. 1808), 80 (Photo No. 3382), 87 (Photo No. 1549).

Cover and book design by Cameron Mason
Edited by Ed Reading

Alaska Northwest Books™
A division of GTE Discovery Publications, Inc.
22026 20th Avenue S. E.
Bothell, Washington 98021

Printed in U.S.A. on acid-free paper

For my friend, Rick Nelson
Lost at sea with the *Eagle*
October 1977

Contents

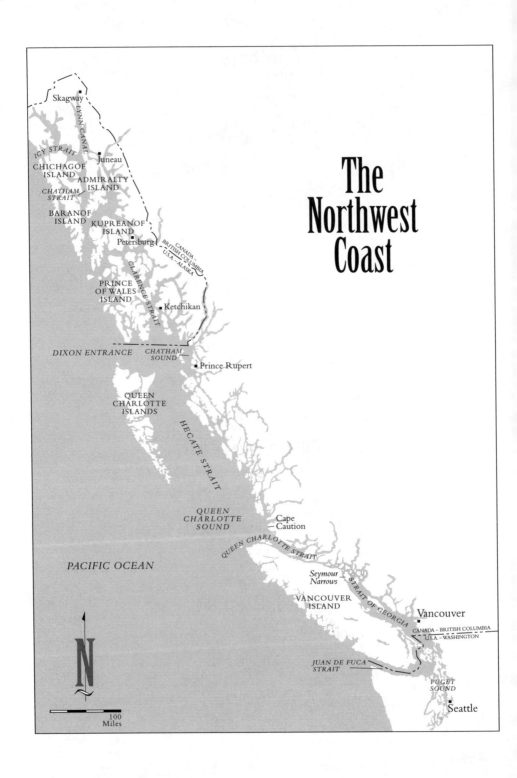

The
Northwest
Coast

Skagway

LYNN CANAL

ICY STRAIT

Juneau

CHICHAGOF
ISLAND

ADMIRALTY
ISLAND

CHATHAM
STRAIT

BARANOF
ISLAND

KUPREANOF
ISLAND

Petersburg

CANADA
BRITISH COLUMBIA
U.S.A. – ALASKA

CLARENCE STRAIT

PRINCE
OF WALES
ISLAND

Ketchikan

DIXON ENTRANCE

CHATHAM
SOUND

Prince Rupert

QUEEN
CHARLOTTE
ISLANDS

HECATE STRAIT

QUEEN
CHARLOTTE
SOUND

Cape
Caution

QUEEN CHARLOTTE STRAIT

Seymour
Narrows

STRAIT OF GEORGIA

VANCOUVER
ISLAND

Vancouver

CANADA – BRITISH COLUMBIA
U.S.A. – WASHINGTON

PACIFIC OCEAN

JUAN DE FUCA
STRAIT

PUGET
SOUND

Seattle

N

100
Miles

Beginnings

~~~

IN THE SPRING of 1965 I was nineteen and helping to bring a 75-foot work boat from Chile to Seattle. On the third day of our forty-day voyage, we stopped for a few hours in the shelter of the desolate guano islands off northern Peru.

There, where convicts had once labored to load sailing ships with the dusty, powdery bird lime, we moved up and down gently in the long swell, pumping fuel from drums on deck to the main tanks below and tightening the rigging. When we were done, we stayed a little longer, enjoying the engineless silence.

The white-haired skipper, Steve Trutich, spread a chart on the hatch and talked about a life spent in another place, the green island wilderness of British Columbia and Alaska. He pointed out places that were to become legends in my mind: Whirlpool Rapids, Hole in the Wall, Icy Strait, Granite Cape, Bay of Pillars, False Pass, Deadmans Sands.

We left Peru and sailed north.

Three weeks later, we anchored off palm-lined beaches in Punta Arenas, Costa Rica. Native skiffs came alongside with spiny lobsters, fruit, and vegetables.

Again the skipper's scarred hands moved over the worn, faded charts, and he pointed to Fords Terror, Wolf Rock, Cholmondeley Sound, Sweetwater Lake, and Tlevak Narrows.

For two weeks more in that spring of 1965 we sailed northward, traveling mostly out of sight of land. We cleared customs in San Diego and passed Cape Mendocino, north of San Francisco, far offshore. North toward Seattle we moved on a blessedly calm Pacific Ocean.

In the flat light of a mean and windy morning, we made out Cape Disappointment and the distant mouth of the Columbia River. Five miles off, our vessel heaved and plunged as the great river's current piled up the seas, and I understood the deathtrap the Columbia and its sand-bar had been for ships. We sailed north.

The next day we came abeam of Fuca Pillar and Tatoosh Island, made our turn east, and entered the fourteen-mile-wide strait that leads to Puget Sound and the maze of inland waterways behind Vancouver Island. The wind was light, the sea calm, the passage easy.

A HARSH HISTORY. It wasn't much of a Christmas for the boys on the big, steel four-master, *Pass of Melfort*. Inbound from Panama to Port Townsend, Washington, she approached the coast after dark in snow and a heavy southeasterly gale. Perhaps she'd overrun her course, traveled farther than her dead reckoning track showed. We'll never know. She drove ashore on Christmas night, 1905, near Amphitrite Point, British Columbia, and all hands were lost.

Nor was fortune kind to the coastal steamer *Valencia* a year later. The skipper thought he was still off the Washington coast when his ship drove onto the rocks near Pachena Point, British Columbia. One hundred seventeen died when the rescue ships were unable to get

Fierce winds and 50-foot seas ripped sails from the **Carelmapu** *in 1915, forcing the Chilean ship onto a reef off Vancouver Island. Only five crewmembers survived the disaster.*

close enough to help.

And pity the men on the Chilean three-master, *Carelmapu*. Inbound to Puget Sound in November 1915 after a long voyage from the nitrate port of Caleta Buena on the desolate Chilean coast, the men longed for liberty in some wide-open port town, such as Tacoma or Seattle.

But November had been stormy, and the tugs that patrolled the entrance to the strait were harbor-bound. The vessel tacked for days before the entrance, looking for a tow. On the afternoon of the twenty-second, a southeast gale came up, blowing out most of her sails, and she began to lose her fight to stay off the Vancouver Island shore. The next morning, with no canvas left, she stopped finally at the edge of the breakers, held there by her anchors.

With no radio, all she could do was fly the distress flags and hope to be seen. The crew had almost given up hope, with *Carelmapu* dragging down onto the rocks, when the steamer *Maquinna* spotted her on the way out of Clayoquot Sound. The *Maquinna's* captain said the seas were the worst he had ever seen, the largest fifty feet high, and he was thinking of turning back when he sighted the stranded *Carelmapu*.

One look and he knew she was doomed. But he maneuvered his ship upwind, dropped his anchors, and started drifting down toward her, using his engines to ease the strain on the anchor chains.

He got within a thousand feet; he dared go no closer. His crew drifted a line down. Then a great sea thundered onto the *Maquinna* and the strain shattered the anchor winches, tearing them off the deck. There was nothing for it but cut the chains and get clear before he lost his vessel. Another great sea carried *Carelmapu* onto the reef. Of the twenty-four persons aboard, five were left when the tide went out, who staggered, bruised and dazed, over the rocks to shore.

REFUGE.   We made Seattle and the crew melted away to their homes. I stayed aboard, seeking work that would take me to Alaska.

The journey had imbued me with a lifelong fascination with the watery canyons and channels that led north from the forty-ninth parallel into British Columbia and Alaska. Steve gave me that.

His stories of a life along the northern coast had created in my mind a mythic place. Even as I hunted the job that would take me there, I could hear in my head the swift tides rushing down lonely passages. I could see the rotting totems and empty Indian lodges in a dripping forest. Icebergs big as city blocks dropped into shining bays. Eagles and ravens watched the white men come.

My Alaska job appeared a few days later, when I hired on as engineer on an Alaska-bound fish-buying vessel that served a fleet of native fishermen.

Day and night we traveled through the island wildernesses of the Inside Passage. Work took us from these sheltered waters to the ocean coast, to Steamboat Bay, Noyes Island, Cape Ulitka, Cape Chirikof, Cape Augustine, Cape Lookout—uninhabited, wild, bleak, lonely.

THE OUTSIDE COAST.   Imagine a channel windblown and fog-shrouded. Imagine a coast with no harbors for hundreds of miles, nothing but beaches and rocks, a thousand-mile graveyard for ships. Imagine the feelings of a captain as he nears this coast after a voyage of four or five thousand miles across the Pacific, days or weeks without a firm fix of position.

That unimaginable shore is the Northwest coast; the channel, fourteen miles wide, is the Juan de Fuca Strait. To the north lies rocky Vancouver Island, as inhospitable a place for ships as there is on this planet. To the south is the Washington coast, only slightly more forgiving.

For decades, "Lost near Cape Flattery without a trace" was a common epitaph. Yet behind the forbidding outer coast lies a network of sheltered channels, the Inside Passage, without which the history and development of this northern coastal country would have been different.

By choosing its route and picking its weather carefully, even the smallest vessel can manage the thousand-mile journey from southern-most Puget Sound, Washington, to northernmost Lynn Canal, Alaska, in relative safety. Natives in canoes, settlers in gas boats and skiffs, gold seekers in tired steamers, and fishermen in all manner of craft have been able to slip north on the Inside Passage.

This is not to say it is a safe or easy passage. Many have come to grief among the rocky islands and channels. Even the well-traveled portion from Seattle to Ketchikan is tortuous: a 650-mile journey of more than 120 separate legs, zigging and zagging through the maze of islands and channels. And that is the deep-water route. Smaller vessels wanting more sheltered waters take a still more intricate course inland through the island archipelagoes. The tide runs hard. The wind is funneled by the land. Sometimes it's foggy. There are many rocks, and a vessel must be navigated well.

But for all that, the advantage of travel in sheltered waters, with so many harbors available, outweighs the need for careful navigation.

HIGHWAY NORTH. My summer journey to Alaska was the first of many along that coast. For much of the 1970s and early 1980s, I was there faithfully in Southeast Alaska. I worked on boats from Garnet Point, down near the British Columbia border, to Skagway, far north on the edge of the Yukon.

On a wooded point near the cove that on a wild night in 1793 had sheltered Captain Vancouver's ships of discovery, my first wife Susanna and I built a cabin.

The forest was primeval, thick, almost impassable. To go to the next

This man, a hand troller, is one of many rich personalities who eke out a living along the hidden coves and rocky shorelines of the Inside Passage.

house or the trading post, we used the outboard. There were no roads. The mail and supply boat came once a week. The neighbors were trappers, loggers, and fishermen. On summer nights we could hear humpback whales blowing in the tide rips outside. On winter mornings there'd be the tracks of mink and marten.

The store, the bar, and the post office rose with the tides on home-made log rafts. There was no phone in that country, no electricity, no school. In the summer, our lives were dictated by the fishing, the tides, and the wind. After fishing came winter, with plenty of time for visiting.

The people I met gave me the stories of their lives and the lives of those before them in that raw, unpeopled country. Traveling, I sought out the seldom-visited places, the hidden coves and little-used, rock-choked channels, the places on the charts where approximate shapes were indicated by dotted lines and marked "unknown." Chance conversations had me steaming for hours through channels I had no charts for, seeking a wild beach, an abandoned settlement, a hot spring.

And so, over the two decades and a half I have been in that country, in all sorts of vessels, large and small, I have begun to fill in the chart I saw for the first time in the islands off Peru.

For the traveler, it is this I want to convey: a sense of what went before, the drama and power of life, the grace and struggle and adventure of people's journeys here.

In my own journeys, if there has been one moment to save, to taste again and again, it would be this:

May 1982, Thurlow, British Columbia. My wife Mary Lou and crew and I have rushed for weeks to get ready, and we leave Seattle with a deck load to stow and a two-page list of jobs to be done. We catch slack water at Devils Hole and Yuculta Rapids at midnight and tie to the wharf at Thurlow an hour later. We need just to rest, to sleep for a few sweet hours before going on: to Whirlpool and Greene Point rapids, on and on, until we get to our cannery in Alaska, 600 miles away.

It is now the hour before dawn.

I get up quietly, stretch my legs, making dark footprints on the frost-covered dock, and walk past the abandoned lodge, past the rusting farm equipment. As I slip back aboard, first light is coming to the wild land around us.

The big Caterpillar rumbles to life. I throw off the lines from the empty dock, get a coffee, and take it up to the flying bridge. I savor the whistle of the turbo, the rush of the tide, the green smell of the woods, the rich smell of the sea.

Heading north.

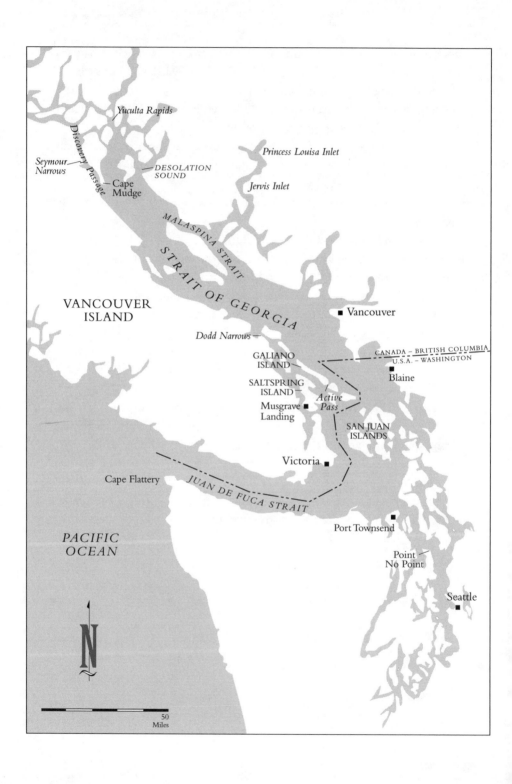

Yuculta Rapids

Princess Louisa Inlet

Seymour
Narrows

Discovery Passage

DESOLATION
SOUND

Jervis Inlet

Cape
Mudge

MALASPINA STRAIT

STRAIT OF GEORGIA

VANCOUVER
ISLAND

Vancouver

Dodd Narrows

CANADA – BRITISH COLUMBIA
U.S.A. – WASHINGTON

GALIANO
ISLAND

SALTSPRING
ISLAND

Blaine

Active
Pass

Musgrave
Landing

SAN JUAN
ISLANDS

Victoria

Cape Flattery

JUAN DE FUCA STRAIT

Port Townsend

PACIFIC
OCEAN

Point
No Point

Seattle

N

50
Miles

CHAPTER ONE

The South End

SEATTLE TO DESOLATION SOUND

WHENEVER A BUNCH OF FELLOWS would get together, someone would start to talking about going up north. . . .

Things were pretty much settled to the south of us. We didn't seem to be ready for steady jobs. It was only natural we'd start talking about the North. We'd bought out the Russians. We'd built canneries up there. The fellows who hadn't been up was hankering to go. The rest of us was hankering to go back.

—Mont Hawthorne, in *The Trail Led North: Mont Hawthorne's Story,* by Martha Ferguson Mckeown

My going-to-Alaska-in-my-own-boat dream ended in the tide rip north of Point Wilson, Juan de Fuca Strait, in June of 1970. I had come to Seattle a month earlier, a young man of twenty-four, to find the salmon gill-net boat *Denise* that I had leased sight-unseen from an acquaintance. He had no photographs, yet he made the *Denise* sound so much like a husky 40-footer that I assumed she was. He marked a chart, showed me the 700-mile marine route north through the islands to Alaska and pointed out the good stopping places to wait when the wind blew.

I had imagined myself up on the flying bridge, grandly steering up the Inside Passage. I'd make a big season up north in the Alaskan wilderness and head south in the fall with a fat wad in my ass pocket, my career begun.

I packed my toolbox and my old duffel and flew across the country from my East Coast home. But when I got to the dock at Fisherman's Terminal in Seattle, I was sure there had been a mistake. Perhaps my boat had been moved, my directions wrong. The sad craft that lay in the slip couldn't possibly be my new command.

Instead of the husky 40-footer I'd come to believe was waiting for me, the 28-foot *Denise* looked like a toy, a kid's version of a real fishing boat, nailed crudely together.

I stepped aboard and she laid over, almost putting her rail under with my weight. The bilge pump started. It was the only thing that worked.

The flying bridge was quarter-inch plywood, impossible to stand on, the interior a tangle of rusty pipes and hanging wires. The engine looked like it belonged in a junk yard.

In the next slip was a boat that was everything mine was not: seaworthy, with a graceful line and shape, the rigging tight, the paint fresh. Her owner stood in the stern, splicing a line. He looked over at me and the *Denise* and summed it up in one sentence:

"I wouldn't let my kid *swim* off that boat."

The smart thing would have been to turn around, to seek Alaska-bound employment on one of the hundreds of nearby vessels then readying to head north.

But I had come so far, and I had told all my friends I had a boat to take north.

I *hungered* to run a boat north, beyond all reason. I hired a mechanic and spent most of my money rebuilding the engine and the boat. On

*The author and his first boat, the **Denise**. The small ship demanded copious supplies of patience, time, and money.*

a warm and fair day, we took her out onto Lake Washington to test the newly rebuilt power plant.

The engine threw a rod, and the poorly insulated exhaust pipe set the boat on fire. The mechanic dove for a fire extinguisher. When we had doused the flames, I dove overboard to cool off and wait for a tow. On the way in, the mechanic turned to me.

"Every one I've rebuilt lately has done that," he said. "I don't understand it."

I could have strangled him.

My money was almost gone. I found another engine, tired but serviceable.

"Plenty of good life left in her," its owner had reassured me. But when I finally got it installed, I found that the rear seal, which is a sort of rubber ring around the crankshaft, was bad. So the engine leaked oil.

A lot of oil. Half a gallon an hour. I couldn't face taking another engine apart, and I was determined to go north. I wedged a fifty-five-gallon drum of cheap, recycled oil into the hold and headed out into Puget Sound, against the advice of family and friends.

When the big steel gates of the Ballard Locks opened up before me, the day had been pleasant, the sea calm, the air warm. The first leg of my journey was smooth, but anxious. I looked for leaks, monitored the engine, and sought out whatever flaws the vessel might have. By Point No Point lighthouse, a marker on a low driftwood-covered spit twenty miles north of Seattle, I began to breathe easier. Aside from the hourly ritual of adding oil to the engine, things seemed to be running more or less smoothly, and I had begun to think of my route, of where to spend the coming night, and of those who had traveled before me.

In the early afternoon, we came to Point Wilson, where the sheltered waters of Puget Sound become the much wider waters of the Juan de Fuca Strait. As we nosed out into the strait on the first leg of our 600-mile trip up the Inside Passage, I felt like the Klondikers of almost three-quarters of a century before, crowding the rail, watching the familiar country fall away behind, seeing the raw, new vistas opening up ahead. I was going to *Alaska!*

The western end of the strait is the North Pacific Ocean, and on many days a westerly arises around noontime in response to the warming of the vast land mass to the east. The westerly pushes against the confused tidal currents near Point Wilson and creates broken water, where seas seem to come from every direction; ships have been lost here.

That day was no different. We got into a tide rip, and I felt the cold metallic taste of fear.

The little *Denise* was pushed one way and then another at the whim of the currents. The sky clouded over; the wind and the tide raised a short, mean chop through which we struggled. Two red lights came on: the bilge pumps. Whether they were gaining or losing I couldn't tell; I couldn't let go of the wheel long enough to see where the water was coming from. Again and again the *Denise* plunged heavily into the trough of a sea, shaking and rattling everything aboard. The engine began to run rough; there was the faint, slightly nauseating smell of gasoline, oil, and filthy bilge water.

A little distance away I glimpsed one of the bigger boats that had moored near me at Fisherman's Terminal. She seemed to be traveling easily through the tide rip, barely wetting her windows, while the *Denise* was fighting for her life.

A few hours later, I made the San Juan Islands and limped into Mackaye Harbor before a raw westerly booming up the strait from the ocean. One thing was clear: to take the *Denise* north would be suicide. My grandly framed Alaska plans had to be put away for another year.

GOLD RUSH. The North beckons, whether for gold, fish, or adventure. Mont Hawthorne, who spoke at the beginning of this chapter about the hankering to go north, lived in Oregon Territory in the 1880s. But the same sentiments are echoed every spring along the Northwest waterfront. There is something about that lonely country that draws one to it.

That day in 1970 when the *Denise* passed Point No Point, the shorelines became hazy, indistinct. The smoky cities that had pushed back the great forests faded, and I imagined another day, in July of 1897, when the steamer *Portland* passed southbound with a ton of gold and set off the great stampede.

News of the gold strike electrified the nation. Thousands of people left Seattle for Alaska and the Yukon in the next six months, many arriving in the middle of winter, unprepared for the rigors that awaited them.

Gold seekers overwhelmed the northbound steamers, and every sort of vessel was pressed into service, including many old and ill equipped.

Two weeks after the *Portland* arrived in Seattle, the steamer *Mexico* left with every berth taken, her decks and holds full of prospectors' supplies. The crowd seeing her off flowed from dock to dock until a mile of waterfront was filled with cheering, envious well-wishers.

Those aboard were lucky; on the return south, the *Mexico* sank in a storm.

The Klondikers left a land where timber was king, where great smoky mills at Port Blakely, Port Gamble, Port Ludlow, and Port Townsend filled windjammers bound for San Francisco and all the

*The discovery of gold on Canada's Klondike River in 1896 unleashed a torrent of fortune-hunters. For the next several years, thousands joined the rush from all over the world. Here the steamship **Victoria** heads north from Seattle, brimming with hopefuls.*

ports on the Pacific. The mill life was a brutal grind for the working-man, and the chance to go north held out the possibility of adventure as well as wealth.

Of course, by the time news of the gold strike in the Yukon made it to Seattle, the best claims had been staked. Those who were to become wealthy were already there.

For most of the '98-ers their first experience at sea was the thousand-mile journey from Seattle to Skagway, their first taste of wide waters at Point Wilson, thirty-five miles out of Seattle.

In the grand houses on the bluff at Port Townsend, south of Point Wilson, ship-watchers that spring must have seen a remarkable sight. In the exodus to the gold rush were twelve identical 176-foot paddle-wheel steamers for Yukon River service. The *J. P. Light, D. R. Campbell, Seattle, Tacoma, Victoria, St. Michael, Pilgrim,* and five others were built side by side in the Moran Shipyards in Seattle to serve the astonishing sudden demand for transport along the Yukon River and tributaries. They and as many more Yukon-bound paddle-wheelers from other yards looked grand with their elegant gingerbread woodwork salons, tall double stacks and long graceful hulls. The smart ones took a northerly course from Point Wilson and followed the Inside Passage as far as they could. The foolhardy turned west, took the straighter, shorter route across the open North Pacific Ocean. Most ships taking this route were severely damaged in the crossing, the low-sided river craft almost totally unsuited for the rigors of the open sea.

DISAPPOINTMENT.   On that first June day when I barely got out of Seattle, I was deeply disappointed at having to give up my Alaska plans, but I had spent all my money. I limped into Blaine, a few hundred yards south of the Canadian border, to piece together a salmon season in Washington state waters.

Gill-netting was a nighttime fishery in Washington. Each evening before I'd leave the harbor, I'd walk to the end of the dock that looked out on the highway to Alaska, the distant Strait of Georgia. Even on good days, when the sun died in brilliant colors over Saturna and Galiano and Vancouver islands, the strait seemed unfriendly, forbidding.

A lot of nights the fish were way out on "the line," the boundary between the United States and Canada. There, the boundary takes a big dogleg right where we need it the most, a big irrational zig in front of the mouth of the Fraser River, where all the fish are headed. It's as if the treaty framers, a hundred and fifty years before, were thinking of us. The other Blaine-based boats had nets much deeper than my Alaska net; my only chance was to fish on the line, where they couldn't set their nets in front of me. And if the night were black enough and the Canadian patrol boats weren't around, we'd turn off our lights and go a little farther and lay out the 1,800-foot net the way white men and natives alike had done it in wooden rowboats before the turn of the century. We'd make a big curving hook toward the west with it and hope that the Fraser River fish would drop down toward U.S. waters as they made their sprint to the spawning grounds.

The day would go from the sky. To the south you could see the glow from the Intalco aluminum plant at Ferndale and the Arco refinery at Cherry Point. To the west was the flash from the lighthouse at East Point, by Boiling Reef in Boundary Pass, and the summer homes on

Saturna, Orcas, and Pender islands, their windows a glistening necklace hung across a great dark void.

To the northeast were the lights of Vancouver, where in 1914 the crack trains of the Canadian Pacific Railway's silk express waited for the steamship *Empress of Russia* to arrive from China. Once loaded with silk, they raced across the continent to East Coast markets.

On a clear night, in every direction except toward the strait, the town lights glowed. The strait was dark, a black gulf, a beckoning road north toward Alaska and the little-populated upcoast of British Columbia.

ACTIVE PASS.　Sometimes, drifting the strait, I'd look to the south and see the lights of Alaska-bound steamers coming up from Puget Sound and making for Active Pass. I would imagine passengers awake in the middle of the night. They'd lie in bed, feel the boat surge from side to side in the tide, as if a great hand were pushing it first one way, then the other, when it entered the pass.

If they were curious, they might dress and go up and forward into one of the salons and peer out at the night. At first they would be startled, for there would be steep shores and lighted windows close on both sides. If it were a clear night, they might look down and see moonlight glimmering on whirlpools, might sense the swirl of powerful currents, and might even have the slightest touch of anxiety for their safety.

As their ship entered the narrows, it would make a hard turn to starboard, a very hard turn, more than ninety degrees. A little later it would make an almost equally hard turn to port.

And finally, the passengers, if their eyes were sharp, would see a green blinking light off to port, and then the boat might begin rolling or pitching, as if it were coming out of a river and into the sea itself. If the chart were handy and the ship's track marked on it, they might see they had come through Active Pass and entered the strait.

A green lad of nineteen, I went through the pass on a 90-foot fish-packing vessel on a morning in June 1965. It was my first trip north.

"Watch this," the skipper said, and I peered where he pointed. One moment there was a solid mass of land ahead, the next a white and blue steamship appeared from a fold in the hills, traveling fast directly toward us.

He spun the wheel hard to starboard, and we sheered off against the current toward the Mayne Island shore until we were traveling on the very edge of the kelp, dangerously close to the shallows.

Still the steamer came, larger and larger, headed right for us. I felt my mouth go dry, my heart begin to pound in my chest. We slid closer to the shore, and the big steamer kept coming.

Time seemed to stop. For one instant, I could look up almost vertically at passengers with startled looks on their faces, holding on as their ship heeled over. At the last moment, her rudder caught hold and she careened off, now alongside us, now lost behind another bend in the channel.

It was over in a minute. But it had been close.

"B.C. ferry," the skipper said finally. "They got to go full steam to keep steerageway with the tide, but all the same, it's an accident waiting to happen."

Five years later, the ferry we had just met, the *Queen of Victoria*, collided in that spot with a Russian freighter, the *Sergey Yesenin*, and three ferry passengers died.

Active Pass is the winding, deep channel between Mayne and Galiano islands, ninety miles north of Seattle; it is the gateway for northbound vessels into the Strait of Georgia and the deep-water route north. It will be a visitor's first experience with the powerful tidal currents of the Northwest coast.

Through this constricted passage and the even narrower ones between the islands to the northwest—Porlier Pass, Gabriola Passage, and Dodd Narrows—pour the tides for most of the lower strait. In a large tide, enough water to raise the level twelve feet must pour through the passes in six hours, an immense volume of water. The currents are enough to bat the largest vessels back and forth. Only in Active Pass is safe passage possible at other than the brief slack period at high or low tide.

If possible, vessels should take Active Pass at slack water; but a vessel with a speed of 10 knots can always get through. If in possession of local knowledge, advantage can be taken of the eddies and variations in the tidal stream; otherwise a vessel should pass through in mid-channel. At all times great care should be taken to avoid the dangers at the western entrance, also to avoid Fairway Bank, and the shoals on either side of the northern entrance to the pass.

On strong flood tides, violent rips, dangerous to boats, occur over an area extending from mid-channel, south of Mary Anne Point, to Laura Point.

—Canadian Hydrographic Service,
Sailing Directions, British Columbia Coast

The Strait of Georgia starts north of the shallows known as Alden Bank in northern Washington. It stretches more than a hundred miles northwest, a twenty-mile-wide inland sea, before losing itself and becoming four different channels between Discovery Passage and Desolation Sound. Its southern end is busy with ship and boat traffic and has settlements and cities on every shore. In the north it ends in roadless wilderness, a land changed little since George Vancouver coasted its shores two hundred years ago.

The strait has a bad reputation among mariners and presents a barrier to small craft. Crossing "the Gulf," as some locals call it—even the relatively short passage from behind Gabriola Island to the first good shelter on the other side—say, Secret Cove—can be an ordeal.

To the west and south are the American San Juans and Canadian Gulf Islands, lying in the rain shadow of the mountains of Vancouver Island. In these islands, travelers northbound in small vessels can experience their last taste of warm southern summer before entering the misty and cooler land to the north.

In May 1972, northbound at last in a new boat after the disastrous *Denise*, I tied to the empty float at Musgrave Landing, on the west side of Saltspring Island. There were no houses in that still and leafy cove, and no other boats, only a wharf and a trail up through the woods. Susanna and I walked along it in shorts, the dog bounding off ahead of us, in and out of the shafts of sunlight that poured through breaks in the forest canopy.

We passed from the cool of the woods into open, sloping fields and the heat of the afternoon. To the west, the land fell away and we looked out at the winding, myriad channels among the islands spread below us.

*Until they were replaced by roomier fiberglass boats in the 1970s,
double-ended gill-netters were common sights in the waterways of
Alaska and British Columbia.*

The sun on our backs felt good and we stayed up on that hillside meadow a long while, knowing that such fair afternoons were uncommon in the region where we were headed.

The strait is open to the full sweep of the prevailing winds, and smaller vessels choose their route with an eye to maximizing travel in protected waters, a route with harbors to duck into should the weather change for the worse.

When it does blow up in the strait, it can get ugly in a hurry. The prevailing westerlies, typically coming up in the early afternoon, make for an uncomfortable cross-chop when opposed by the tidal current, and a strong southeast or northwest gale, blowing down the full length of the strait, can be formidable for even large vessels. In such conditions, any harbor is a good harbor.

The black of the night, the howl of the wind, the slash of the rain, the uncomfortable feel of a boat struggling in a seaway are things that press heavily on a mariner's mind. There are few things better than a good harbor after a hard thrash, few things worse than a bad night on the water.

At such times, even the mariner in a big boat might succumb to the temptation to try one of the narrower passes, to seek the sheltered waters beyond. The bottoms of the passes are littered with the pieces of vessels that have elected to try them in such conditions.

GABRIOLA PASSAGE, being narrow and intricate, with numerous dangers in its eastern approach, is not recommended for general navigation, and should be used only by vessels with local knowledge.

—*Sailing Directions*

"What could I have done? It was a smoking southeasterly . . . seem like it just came up right out of nowhere. Comin' on dark, jes' something about the wind and the night, like they *push* a fella, you know what I mean? I just couldn't stand the thought of spending a night out in the gulf on the slow bell, just joggin' into it, always worryin' for the queer one that was waiting to punch a window out. And I'd been through Gabriola two, three times, anyway, so I figured I knew the lay of the land pretty good. If it looked like the tide was running too fast, I'd just slip in behind Breakwater Island, drop the hook, get out of the weather that way. It felt so good to just turn and run before it, get out of the trough of them seas. Who would have thought it could get so dark so fast, or that the wind'd be pushin' the tide through them holes like water down a funnel? There's no lights through there . . . all there was to go by was the gleam of the breaking water in the tide rips. But that current! By the time I thought about swinging in behind the island, instead of going through, it was too late, that current had a hold of me, and there weren't nothing to do but shoot on through . . . Well, I kept her in the middle and we got through all right, but I never thought it'd be that bad, just sucking you in like that."

—A friend

And I was no less foolish one October night. It was my sixth season of running vessels up and down the Inside Passage and working in Southeast Alaska. I considered myself experienced.

That night, we were operating a 65-footer towing a disabled 36-foot gill-netter. The last of the light found us in the Strait of Georgia with a wind rising and the weather report poor.

The coming of dark and the push of the wind made me anxious, eager for sheltered waters. And so, rather than face a long buck down the strait in the black, I turned south and entered Northumberland Channel. Ahead was a slot between two islands, beyond which lay a channel where the wind reached but little. If we could make it through, we might be able to continue our homeward journey.

The radio spoke.

"Gonna try it, eh . . . ?" It was our friend at the end of the tow line. He had tried to make his voice neutral, yet underneath I sensed apprehension. He was speaking of Dodd Narrows, the constricted passage ahead. A gorge between rocky banks, through which the current runs extremely rapidly, it wasn't much of a spot to try in the black of night, especially when the tide had turned against us.

> Dodd Narrows . . . Under ordinary circumstances, it is considered that Dodd Narrows should not be attempted by any vessel whose length exceeds 150 feet, and local knowledge is a requirement. To short, handy power vessels, the passage presents no dangers at or near slack water, or when proceeding in the direction of the tidal stream; *but no attempt should be made to pass through against the tidal stream.*
> —*Sailing Directions* (emphasis added)

Yet sheltered waters lay beyond; we could continue our journey regardless of the weather outside.

"Oh . . . I dunno," I said. "Think we can get through?"

"Late on the tide, aren't we?"

I looked at the tide book. He was right; slack water had passed ninety minutes earlier; the current would be running strongly against us.

"Maybe it won't be that bad . . . what d'you think?"

There was a long silence, then, "Sometimes it's bad . . . "

I knew what he was thinking: that a prudent sailor would have snuggled over to the shore, perhaps tied to one of the many log rafts moored to the side of Gabriola Island and waited for daylight and slack water.

But even inside the boat we could hear the rumble of the machinery at the giant pulp mill at Harmac. After the North Country it wouldn't be a very peaceful anchorage. And more, I had corral fever; I just wanted to get home.

"Aw, what the heck," I finally said. "Let's go for it . . . you only go around once."

I slowed down to an idle and called on the radio again.

"Maybe I'll shorten up that tow line a bit," I joked. "I'd hate to scrape you off over a thin place."

We brought him in until he trailed barely fifty feet astern. If it had been light, I'd *never* have tried it, but it being black and all, I couldn't see how hard the current was running, until it was too late. I got up on the flying bridge and had my engineer handle the big spotlight.

We snuck along the Vancouver Island shore, staying out of the stream until we were almost in the narrows, and then I throttled up and we shouldered our way out into the current.

Instantly, I knew it was a *bad* mistake—the tide was running much faster than I had anticipated, boiling through the gap.

But by then we were committed; trying to turn around would have been as risky as proceeding. I pushed the throttle all the way against the governor stop and hoped for the best.

Right off the current sheered us off to port until our rigging was brushing the trees. I turned the wheel violently the other way, but the boat seemed not to respond at all. In the light of the spotlight I could see rocks, almost beneath our bow. Then suddenly the rudder grabbed hold and we lurched off the other way, careening across the channel and heading for the trees as I spun the wheel. Again and again I turned the wheel hard-over one way, then hard-over the other way, fighting to stay off the rocks, my heart in my throat.

It seemed to go on for hours, but of course it was only a few minutes, and then we were under the power lines and through the gap, and my heart started beating again. My shirt was soaked right through with sweat, yet the night was almost cold.

I called back to my friend on the tow. He was a cool customer, experienced in all manner of craft, big and small, and in his twenty-fifth season in the North.

"Oh," he answered offhandedly, "it wasn't that bad. I had to steer a little bit there, to keep off the beach, you know . . . "

"O.K.," I said, "just checking on you. It was a little worse than I figured, but what the hell . . . we made it, right?"

"Yup," he said, "we made it, all right." He paused. "And, oh yeah, I bit my cigar in half."

While the steamers, tugs, and big fish boats travel around the clock in the Inside Passage, small commercial boats bound for upcoast British Columbia and Alaska only travel in daylight hours, constrained by small crews and the constant danger of logs and deadheads in the water.

In May and June, when there are almost twenty hours of daylight, the trip can go quickly, but in the fall, when the weather is frequently bad and night comes early, each leg of the trip is apt to be shorter.

VANCOUVER. June of 1792 saw the English explorer, Captain George Vancouver, in the Strait of Georgia, mapping, naming, and exploring. Historians have called Vancouver the first explorer of Puget Sound and coastal British Columbia. Yet at the time of his arrival, the native people had a sophisticated culture and trade routes up and down the coast. Eager to obtain highly valued sea otter pelts from the natives, the whites offered in trade a variety of goods of varying usefulness. They also brought pestilence and death; many tribes shrank substantially from smallpox and other diseases brought by the white men.

Vancouver's remarks upon entering the Puget Sound country for the first time are accurate today:

> The serenity of the climate, the innumerable pleasing landscapes, and
> the abundant fertility that unassisted nature puts forth, require only to
> be enriched by the industry of man with villages, mansions, cottages,
> and other buildings, to render it the most lovely country that can be
> imagined; whilst the labor of the inhabitants would be amply
> rewarded in the bounties which nature seems ready to bestow on
> cultivation.
>
> —George Vancouver, *A Voyage of Discovery*
> *to the North Pacific Ocean and Around the World*

Vancouver's goal was to find a sea route to the Atlantic, a Northwest Passage, the fabled Strait of Anian. After determining that no such passage lay in Puget Sound, he worked northward, concentrating his efforts in the Strait of Georgia.

Concerned with the extraordinary amount of coastline before him, and the shortness of the season, Vancouver anchored his ships, the *Chatham* and the *Discovery*, in Birch Bay, northern Washington, and sent Lieutenant Joseph Whidbey to explore to the southeast with the *Discovery*'s cutter and the *Chatham*'s launch. He provisioned two other small craft with a week's supplies and set off with Lieutenant Peter Puget and a crew of seamen to explore to the north.

They soon met natives in Burrard Inlet, from whose behavior they surmised themselves to be the first white men the natives had ever seen. Much of the country was so steep the explorers were forced to sleep in the boats for lack of places to set up their tents.

Inlet by inlet, channel by channel, they went, naming, charting, seeking, hoping at every turn to find the passage sought for so long.

The second inlet they explored was Howe Sound, one of a series of deep and winding channels that plunge into the rugged interior, very different from the Puget Sound country to the south.

> The low fertile shores we had accustomed to see, though lately with some interruption, here no longer existed; their place was now occupied by the base of the stupendous snowy barrier, thinly wooded, and rising from the sea abruptly to the clouds; from whose frigid summit the dissolving snow in foaming torrents rushed down the sides and chasms of its rugged surface, exhibiting altogether a sublime, though gloomy spectacle, which animated nature seemed to have deserted. Not a bird, nor living creature was to be seen, and the roaring of the falling cataracts in every direction precluded their being heard, had any been in our neighborhood.
>
> —Vancouver, *A Voyage of Discovery*

Their hopes were raised two days later when they entered Jervis Inlet, which winds for forty miles into the heart of the mountains. From the depth and width of the channel, and the direction it appeared to be leading, they began to think once again they had found the Northwest Passage.

On the eighteenth of June in the early evening, the channel ended in a swampy lowland. Discouraged and low on food, they turned back to their ships, pausing only to sleep for a few hours, to fish, or to barter for food.

Vancouver assumed he was the first white man to explore these waters. Imagine his surprise when he and his men rowed small boats down the east side of the strait, near the present site of the University of British Columbia, Vancouver, and found two Spanish ships anchored. Furthermore, the Spaniards, Commanders Galiano and Valdes, showed him a partial chart of the region they had made the previous year. Not only was Vancouver surprised at their presence, he was astonished (his word) at the small vessels they were using. International rivalries set aside, they had lunch and shared information.

In Jervis Inlet, Vancouver had missed the gorge now known as Malibu Rapids, which leads to dramatic and popular Princess Louisa Inlet, the destination of choice for many Northwest yachtsmen. The inlet extends four miles northeast from the rapids. A kind of Yosemite of the North, it is a dramatic canyon, surrounded by mountains rising steeply to six and eight thousand feet, and with a graceful cascade, Chatterbox Falls, at its head.

His men also didn't see or didn't explore Sechelt Inlet. It is just as well, for the rapids at the entrance in Skookumchuck Narrows might have sucked them in before they realized their danger. Skookumchuck is Chinook (an Indian trading jargon) for strong, mighty waters. Anyone who misread his tide book and blundered into its ten-foot overfalls and standing waves would probably agree. Even from the safety of shore, the power of the water thundering through the narrow channel is a sobering sight; the Canadian pilot book remarks, "This causes the formation of the furious and dangerous Sechelt Rapids, the roar of which is audible for many miles."

If there is a bad place in the strait, one that truly stands waiting for the unwary, it is on the western side, near the Vancouver Island shore at Cape Mudge. Known locally as the Graveyard, it is a place where a vessel can pass within a few hundred yards from calm and sheltered waters into a maelstrom that smaller craft may not survive.

The bad part about the Graveyard is it comes upon you so suddenly. A southbound vessel leaving the sheltered channels north of Cape Mudge might not fully appreciate the strength of the wind blowing in

*The steamer **Northwestern** aground in Wrangell Narrows in 1919. The hardy ship endured 18 groundings up and down the coast, finally succumbing to a Japanese bomb in Dutch Harbor during World War II.*

the strait and, furthermore, might be taking advantage of the south-flooding tide to pick up a little speed.

> CAUTION—Off Cape Mudge, and between it and Willow Point, there is a heavy race on the south-going tidal streams, which, when opposed by strong southeasterly winds, set up steep and heavy seas which are dangerous to small craft. Under such conditions small vessels are therefore advised to pass through the area at or after high water slack.
>
> —*Sailing Directions*

The vessel would come around the point with the tide behind it, traveling quite rapidly, and be in a violent tide rip, with extremely short, steeply breaking seas on all sides. The current would push the vessel farther and farther into the rip and away from safety.

What happens here happens quickly. The steam tug *Petrel* got into the rip two nights after Christmas in 1952, and the men on board didn't even have time for a call on the radio. She went down in 70 fathoms with all hands.

Fortunately for the steamer *Northwestern*, when she lost her way on a snowy December night in 1927 and stranded near Cape Mudge, the southerly gale wasn't blowing. For the natives and settlers on nearby Quadra Island, the stranding was an unexpected Christmas present, for the vessel was loaded with all sorts of Alaska-bound Christmas goodies. As soon as she was abandoned, they took advantage of the situation to lighten her load.

Before the development of electronic aids such as radar and depth sounders, ships on the Alaska run had more than a nodding acquaintance with the shore. The *Northwestern* found herself on the bottom eighteen different times up and down the coast, refloated each time, until the Japanese bombed her down for good in the Aleutians in 1942.

NORTH OF THE STRAIT.   Vancouver had remarked on the change in vegetation from one end of the strait to the other. Deciduous trees—arbutus or madrona, birch, maple, and the like—are fairly common in the Gulf Islands, the San Juans, and around Puget Sound, but more scarce as you go north. By the time you get to Desolation Sound or north into Johnstone Strait, about the only time you'll see stands of hardwoods is where the softwood forests have been cleared for a cannery or homestead and alders have grown up in their place, or where a thoughtful pioneer planted apple or perhaps even maple trees.

In the fall especially, north of the Strait of Georgia it is common to travel for miles and miles along dark evergreen–clad shores and suddenly come around a point and be surprised at a splash of color. A traveler not in a hurry might anchor and go ashore, to find a tumble-down cabin or little farm, the apples or maples in bright fall plumage, tribute to a long-dead homesteader. The woods grow back, and homes, cabins, or even whole towns abandoned are overgrown by the forest.

In 1971 in a small sailboat, I stopped at the government float at Redonda Bay, Desolation Sound. The settlement the wharf was built to serve was gone, and the few buildings still standing on the beach were in disrepair. Yet it was a graceful, magic place, and we wandered in the tall grass, going to windowless buildings, listening to the cry of birds and the distant thunder of the tide in Hole in the Wall rapids. Once the summer home of the Salish Indians, the little bay had seen the ebb and flow of fisheries and logging ventures.

Hand loggers made up the first wave of commerce along the north coast, arriving in the 1870s and 1880s. Working largely without machinery, except for hand screw jacks to move felled trees, these men liked to cut trees in places where they could be skidded easily down into the salt water. This steep inlet country was just what they were looking for, and the little store here was the only dot of civilization for many miles.

Fisheries were next, with the Redonda Canning and Cold Storage Company in operation by 1922. Those pre-Depression years were busy in the region; the Redonda Bay store supplied fishing and logging camps in all the remote bays and arms. The paddle-wheel ferry SS *Transfer*, built in 1893 for Fraser River service, was drug ashore here, her boiler providing power for the cannery and her staterooms housing Chinese workers. The lights of the little settlement blazed all night long, quite an unusual thing in those days.

But the Depression hit hard, and the logging and fishing operations closed; only the store remained open. A decade passed. The cannery started up again, and logging was extended into the valleys with trucks and tractors. In the 1940s and early 1950s, the bay became the stopover place for vessels waiting for the tide at Yuculta Rapids. Then refrigerated fish-buying vessels arrived to take the fish to canneries in the big towns and put the little canneries out of business. The Redonda Bay plant closed in 1956, followed by the store eight years later. By the late 1960s the bay was abandoned and silent.

In the fall of 1972, we stopped again, southbound from Alaska. The float was gone, towed away, we heard, by a homesteader, and the buildings had deteriorated. But after a long season in green-gray Southeast Alaska, we lingered there, walking among the ruins, struck by the muted reds and yellows on a rainy October afternoon.

Three years later I returned. By that time, the buildings had fallen into the bay. A big bulldozer was clearing land; a barge had landed half a dozen ugly trailers on the beach. It would be a minimum security prison camp, where the prisoners would work in the forest, thinning trees. Only the bright foliage on the maples, birches, alders, and apple trees spoke of what had been there before.

It is not uncommon in the strait for a windy, rainy southeaster to last for days. For a small boat, what may have been an easy downwind run before a warm breeze, perhaps from the Gulf Islands to Jervis Inlet or Princess Louisa Inlet, or north to Desolation Sound, can become a long and rough buck against the wind and sea on the return. It was that way for a lady and me in a rented 26-foot sailboat in 1971.

August 22, Vananda Cove, B.C. Oh, mean and dreary place! Left Refuge Cove [Desolation Sound] at 7:00 A.M. this morning and bucked all day for twenty-five measly miles, and every one fought for. Malaspina Strait, in the grim late afternoon light, seemed somehow mean, bleak, and unfriendly, and the prospect of being caught out after dark, unthinkable. So ducked into this open cove, tied at the government float to try and get relief from the swell coming in from the open strait. The prospect of another two days like this one to get down into the Gulf Islands is depressing.   —Log

After supper the wind swung and drove in a swell; we started to pound heavily against the float. With the rain lashing our oilskins, we moved the boat around to the inside of the float. In the black and the rain, I didn't realize we had tied the boat under the dock, at low tide.

The tide began to come up when we were asleep. I woke to an odd booming sound, and the whole boat shuddered. I got up groggily and looked outside, becoming suddenly horrified at what was happening. The top of our mast was jammed into the dock above it, and the rising tide was forcing our boat deeper into the water. Moving quickly, I untied the lines and shoved the boat away from the dock. We heeled over violently, but, with a lurch and a shower of splinters, we came free. The lady was really impressed with my seamanship.

This was the cove into which the sinking Union Steamship Company vessel *Cheslakee* staggered on a January night in 1913. A heavy gale was roaring out in the strait, and the *Cheslakee* was hit by two great seas, one after the other, and began to founder. In the cove was the mining community of Van Anda, the nearest shelter. The ship just made it to the wharf before sinking, but three people were lost in the confusion.

Today Vananda Cove and the northern end of the Strait of Georgia mean something very different for the southbound mariner: civilization.

For the most part, the land to the north is wilderness. The coast road on the mainland ends at Lund, just south of Desolation Sound, cut off by the mountains that drop in places almost vertically into the water. In most anchorages to the north, there are no lights on shore, no houses, no noise except the wind or perhaps the rush of a creek tumbling into the salt water.

West of Cape Mudge on the Vancouver Island shore is the big sawmill at Campbell River. On the other side, at Powell River, is the MacMillan-Bloedel and Powell River Company pulp and paper mill complex, an immense facility, one of the largest in the world.

For the southbound traveler, it is the lights and noise from these two plants, carrying many miles into the strait, that herald entry to civilization.

October 26, 1975, Stuart Island, B.C. Laid in to this little wharf in the late afternoon, our nineteenth day en route from Haines, Alaska. We made the lines fast to the float and shut all down, walked up the ramp to shore, the sudden silence ringing in our ears. The sleepy fishing resort was closed for the season, but a kindly owner opened the showers, and for a long time we soaked, feeling the cares of the 140 days since we'd left Seattle fade away. Afterwards we walked to the light at Harbott Point. To the south, looming faintly in the purple evening light, were the graceful shapes of the Rendezvous Islands and the wink of the light on West Redonda that marked the way to Lewis Channel and Desolation Sound. It was our last night before we entered the Strait of Georgia, the light, the noise, the congestion of the busy south coast. It had been a long season, and I had much to do upon returning. Yet these few miles of country were among my favorite on the whole coast, and I felt like lingering. By tomorrow night, the land would be very different, the wilderness behind us. It was as if, even after so long away, the spell of the North wouldn't let go. —Log

We had finished our season that year in the shadow of the great glaciers, at the head of Lynn Canal. For the last week, there had been snow on deck in the mornings, ice in the dog's bowl. One would think a person would be ready for a house, perhaps, be eager to get off the boat. Yet after almost five months in the North, I was reluctant to steam the last miles and enter the very different world that lay ahead, to leave the wilderness behind.

There are fewer towns and services north of the Strait of Georgia, and travelers must fend for themselves, like those on the Canadian troller in Teakerne Arm in 1972:

> "One fall we laid into Talbot Cove—you know where it is, on the south side of Teakerne Arm. We had a couple of hours to kill, waiting on the tide at the Yucultas, so we tied to the log boom there. A couple of big Canadian West Coast trollers were there, and I got to visiting with one of the guys. All of a sudden there was this sound from one of the boats, like a woman crying out. The Canadian excused himself and disappeared for a while into the boat. When he came out, he was wiping his hands on a rag. It almost looked like blood, and I asked him what was going on.
>
> "'Oh,' he said nonchalantly, 'that was the baby coming out.' He shrugged. 'It was a girl.'"
>
> —A friend

Ironically, the area known as Desolation Sound, which so depressed Captain Vancouver in 1792, has become one of the more popular destinations for Northwest boaters able to make the trip. The warm water, dramatic views, and intricate, remote, unspoiled harbors account for the region's popularity. The tides from Johnstone Strait to the north and the Strait of Georgia to the south meet there; in the summer the water is the warmest in the region.

Of course, Vancouver's first night in the area was enough to sour anyone. It was black and rainy, and the English were traveling in company with the Spanish vessels they had met earlier. The little flotilla drifted around in water too deep to anchor, at the mercy of shifting winds and currents. Finally, around midnight, they managed to anchor in some 32 fathoms, near what is now called Kinghorn Island.

The next day a hard southerly came up, and the fleet quickly drug off into deep water. Luckily, by then, Lieutenant Broughton had returned in a small boat with the news of a better anchorage, and they scudded before the storm to the shelter of Teakerne Arm.

Possibly Vancouver's feelings were colored by persistent disappointment in his search for the passage to the east. He had had a long talk with the Spaniards about their travels, and what he heard was not

*Fearsome tides and changeable weather complicated the passage of Captain George Vancouver. The expedition's large ships could not easily make their way through labyrinthine channels, and in 1792, the **Discovery** went on the rocks in Queen Charlotte Sound.*

encouraging, for the Spaniards told him that none of the natives, and none of the American and British fur traders at Nootka on the outside coast of Vancouver Island, had ever spoken of such a passage.

Whatever the reason, his feelings about the region were plain when he wrote:

> Our residence here was truly forlorn; an aweful silence pervaded the gloomy forests, whilst animated nature seemed to have deserted the neighboring country, whose soil afforded only a few small onions, some samphire, and here and there bushes bearing a scanty crop of indifferent berries. Nor was the sea more favorable to our wants, the steep rocky shores prevented the use of the seine, and not a fish at the bottom could be tempted to take the hook.
>
> —Vancouver, *A Voyage of Discovery*

Vancouver's gloom may not have been shared by his men. The expedition botanist, Archibald Menzies, spoke of the men going to the nearby waterfall every day and using it like a resort, while their captain was writing such cheerless reports.

These were exciting times for the ordinary seamen who were exploring in the small boats, although it's possible they didn't think so at the time. Vancouver's ships, *Discovery* and *Chatham,* were simply too big and difficult to maneuver in the constricted waters, so the exploration was done in small boats. Near Toba Inlet, while investigating an Indian village, the explorers were so beset by fleas they jumped into the water for relief and ended by boiling their clothes. At Arran Rapids, at the mouth of Bute Inlet, the current was so strong against them they needed help from the natives to pull their boats through with ropes from the shore.

Some of these men possibly had been with Captain Cook: Vancouver had been. They had been more than halfway way around the world before they got to the northwest coast of America. They had island-hopped through the Pacific and wintered over at Hawaii, and they were just ordinary people from the coast of England.

What must they have thought, exploring, hoping each new turn in the immense archipelago would lead to the Northwest Passage, or worrying that it might instead be a tidal maelstrom? If they knew how to write, no chatty letters survived.

Still, across the centuries, aren't awe and wonder universal expressions of the human spirit? Wouldn't awe have filled these men?

The navigation, exploration, and charting of the myriad channels in this area was one of the challenging parts of Vancouver's five-year voyage. The tides are violent, the weather fickle. The channels wind around with no seeming plan or reason. Reefs and rocks await the careless.

Yet the charts the voyagers produced were remarkable in their accuracy. In the 1950s a Canadian frigate was dispatched from her base near Victoria, the southernmost city along this coast, to an inlet 500 miles to the north. The regular charts were locked away, and the officers used only Vancouver's Great Chart, which he had made from his surveys. The vessel was instructed to proceed through inside waters only, both to and from her destination. She made the 1,000-mile round trip without incident, a tribute to the efforts of Vancouver and his men almost 170 years before.

It was the tides that led Vancouver's boat crews to believe that the channels leading northwest through the maze of islands led to the ocean. Lieutenants Puget and Whidbey had returned from the west side of the strait reporting a channel leading northwest, from which the flood tide poured into the strait. Before this, the tides flooded from the south, from the Juan de Fuca Strait.

About this time, Lieutenant James Johnstone and his men, who were exploring channels to the northwest of Desolation Sound, had the odd experience of the tide being high when they had expected it to be low. They were asleep at the time, on the shore of what is now called Loughborough Inlet, when the rising water began lapping at them. Johnstone quickly grasped that the only possible explanation was that the flood was coming from the Pacific, northwest, rather than through the strait, southeast.

Determined to test his theory, and leaving many promising inlets and channels for later exploration, Johnstone set out through the widest channels, hoping to get a glimpse of the ocean before dwindling supplies forced him to turn around.

On the tenth of July, 1792, almost 120 miles from the ships and with little food left, Johnstone and his crew were rewarded with a distant view of the ocean. What they saw was actually Queen Charlotte Sound, but the important thing was, they had determined all the land west of them to be an island, so they could continue their explorations to the north. With that discovery, they headed back before a westerly gale on the strait that bears Johnstone's name.

Vancouver speaks of his men's journeys for the most part without adjectives, except in describing the land or the weather, as if the work was without hardship, challenge, or danger. All mariners know better.

In May 1973, northbound to Alaska, we laid over at a rotting float at the abandoned settlement of Owen Bay, off Okisollo Channel, west of Desolation Sound.

Deep in the night I awoke and went out on deck trying to place the sound of distant thunder, for the night was clear. Then I realized what it was: the tide, billions of gallons of water, was pouring through Hole in the Wall and the rapids just to the north, making the earth shake with the violence of its passage.

We were traveling in a diesel-powered fiberglass boat, towing a skiff deeply laden with supplies. We had charts, tide tables, radar, radios, a stove, and all the food we wanted. Yet I worried about making a safe passage.

In such moments, I think of Vancouver and his men in those same waters in open boats, with nothing but their eyes and their hands. Running low on food, they pressed ever northward, seeking the Northwest Passage.

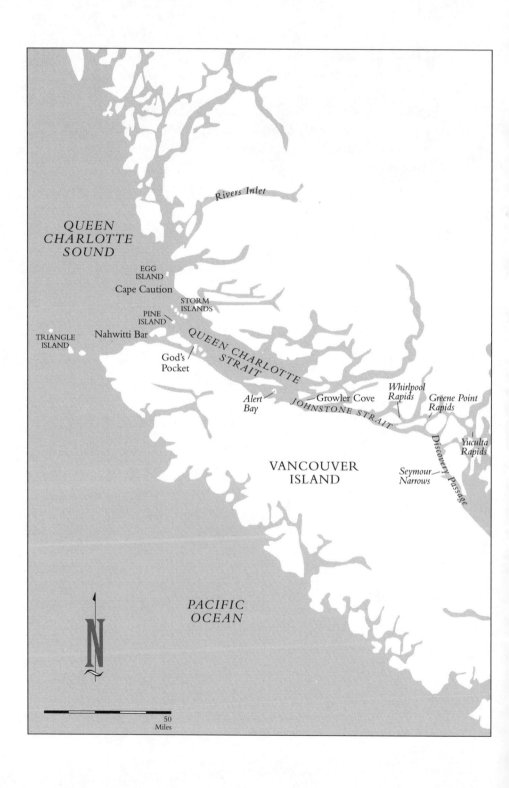

QUEEN
CHARLOTTE
SOUND

Rivers Inlet

EGG
ISLAND
Cape Caution
STORM
ISLANDS
PINE
ISLAND
TRIANGLE
ISLAND
Nahwitti Bar

QUEEN CHARLOTTE STRAIT

God's
Pocket

Alert
Bay

JOHNSTONE STRAIT

Growler Cove

Whirlpool
Rapids

Greene Point
Rapids

Yuculta
Rapids

Seymour
Narrows

Discovery Passage

VANCOUVER
ISLAND

PACIFIC
OCEAN

N

50
Miles

CHAPTER TWO

The Wilderness Begins

SEYMOUR NARROWS TO
QUEEN CHARLOTTE SOUND

UP A PIECE ABOVE VANCOUVER we came to Seymour Narrows. I'd heard about it being a dirty piece of water, so I stayed on deck to study it. It's got to be run when there is slack water, on account of the strong tide. If you are off a half hour either way, you can't go through until the tide changes. We had to lay off there awhile waiting, and I had a chance to talk to one of the pilots about the narrows. He said it was a terrible place to navigate. There's a sucking whirlpool. I can tell you how it works. It's just like pulling the plug and letting the water run out of the bath tub. The farther down it gets, the more it whirls round and round. Then it gets just like a funnel with all the water pushing and shoving to get into the whirl. That's what happens when it's high tide and the water fills in between

[Vancouver Island] and the mainland.

The pilot told me that an English man-of-war started through, and the tide caught him. Some fellows over on the island claimed they seen the boat when it first got caught in the whirl. He went around faster and faster, until he was sucked down clean out of sight. Yes, sir, they never even seen so much as a draw bucket come floating to the surface. Even the masts went down in that hole. It was just the end for every soul on board. Well, after he got done telling me about it, we waited awhile, then we got the signal, and we run slow bell right through them narrows, and we never had a mite of trouble, neither.

—Mckeown, *The Trail Led North*

It is no secret along the waterfront what happens to the unwary or unfortunate at Seymour Narrows. The tide runs faster there than most men can run, the channel takes a right-angle turn, and at one time a pinnacle rock rose out of deep water right in the narrowest part of the channel.

Through it passed most coastal traffic and Alaska-bound steamers. The passes to the north and east are too rock-choked and too narrow for larger vessels. And so travelers approached the narrows at the northern end of the Strait of Georgia with a certain amount of apprehension.

The cautions in *Sailing Directions* show the danger:

In Seymour Narrows, the tidal streams attain velocities up to 15 knots, the flood setting southward, and the ebb in the opposite direction. When either stream is running at strength, the eddies and swirls are extremely heavy, and when opposed by a strong wind, the races become very dangerous to small vessels.

The size of the whirlpools, the violence of the rips, and the depth of the overfalls are legendary. Vancouver had been impressed:

The tide, setting to the southward through this confined passage, rushes with such immense impetuosity as to produce the appearance of falls considerably high.

In 1875, the U.S. warship *Wachusett* was caught in a whirlpool there and destroyed. Over the next eighty years twenty-four ocean-going vessels and more than a hundred smaller ones were to be lost or damaged either by the violent tide rips or by the pinnacle, Ripple Rock.

The rock was the top of a ridge rising out of 400 feet of water. Its position and orientation created such violent eddies that sometimes even large vessels were thrown against it. It was under water, so you couldn't see exactly where it was, and the tide ran so hard and the channel was so narrow there that the rock couldn't be safely buoyed or marked.

Although safe passage was possible only at slack water, slack lasted for ten minutes, perhaps twenty at the outside, and came only every six hours. Vessels that went through after the current had begun to run ran afoul of Old Rip or the eddies and whirlpools.

THE BLAST AT RIPPLE ROCK. As the toll of lost and damaged vessels continued to mount in the twentieth century, planners began to wonder about how to remove the rock, speculating that if they were to remove enough of it, perhaps the worst of the eddies and whirlpools might be reduced also.

The only opposition to such a plan came from railroad interests and businessmen at Victoria, on the southern tip of Vancouver Island. Before their plans were dashed by the daunting terrain in the Desolation Sound area, they had hoped to bring the railroad to their city from the mainland with a series of bridges. Ripple Rock figured in their plans as a support for a bridge across Seymour.

In 1943, drilling and blasting from a specially designed barge was attempted. Moored with six giant concrete anchors, two of 250 tons and four of 150 tons, the barge was held in position over Ripple Rock with heavy cables. But even the immense anchors were no match for the currents, and work was all but impossible. The drillers would start a hole, drill a few feet, then the barge would shift and the drill bit would break or pull out of the hole.

The problem was more than just keeping the barge in one spot— the strain caused the cables to vibrate so badly that they soon parted. Next, engineers drove thick steel bolts into holes drilled into bedrock on the shore, and they moored the barge with cables from shore.

The force of the current was so great that the cables would vibrate until the specially forged bolts would shear off after a few days. The British Columbia Bridge and Dredging Company hung two thick steel cables, 3,500 feet long, across the narrows, and they tried mooring the barge to the overhead cables. But the swirling and unpredictable currents allowed only short periods of drilling each day during slack water, and several workmen drowned when their work skiff capsized and the current pulled them quickly out of reach. It became obvious that working from a barge was too hazardous and too slow, and that tactic was abandoned. Almost a decade passed before another approach was tried.

"Well, we got down towards Seymour, and we were way late on the tide, but it didn't look as if he was gonna pull in anywhere and wait. So I sez, 'Say, Bill, yer not gonna run Seymour, are you now?' 'Got to, Kenny,' sez he, and right then I knew we were in for it.

"Man, I want to tell you the tide was running like a bullet, and I went up on the flying bridge with him, and you could see boats ducked into little holes along the shore, waiting for slack water, and all the gangs on the boats were waving violently to us to stop, to pull in and wait. But Skipper, he wasn't going for it and then it was too late and we were in it, just like that.

"We'd have lost the big skiff for sure, if she hadn't been chained down. Sometimes the whole boat'd drop six or eight feet into one of those holes, and she'd lay way over one way, put her rail right under water, and then lay right over the other way.

"Swirl around? I guess we did, two or three times, anyway, completely around, 360 degrees, and the engine going for all she was worth all the time too. That was when Ripple Rock was right in the middle of the worst place, before they blasted it the hell out of there, and the current, she liked to rush us right against it. And all so quick, three-four minutes at the most and we were through the worst of it.

"We made it, and Bill, he got to see his wife before she died, that's what we was rushing down fer, but I couldn't go with him no more after that. It wasn't right, you know, taking a chance like that with the gang aboard and all, it wasn't right."

—A friend

A massive explosion decimated Ripple Rock in Seymour Narrows,
for centuries the scourge of mariners. Miners tunneled thousands of feet
from the nearby shore to place charges for the 1958 blast, which spewed
400,000 tons of rock into the air.

In 1953, almost eighty years after Ripple Rock had claimed its first
major ship, a test hole was drilled under the narrows. An examination of
the core showed that the integrity of the rock would allow a major tun-
neling and mining project under it to blow it up.

First, a 570-foot vertical shaft was sunk on Maude Island, the east
shore. Next, a 2,400-foot horizontal tunnel was drilled and blasted to a
point the engineers hoped was directly beneath Ripple Rock. Then,
working with extreme caution and always exploring ahead with small-
diameter diamond drills, the team excavated two vertical shafts 300 feet
up into the twin pinnacles of Ripple Rock.

Inside Ripple Rock itself, just beneath the roaring tides, the miners,
who were now at the end of 3,300 feet of narrow tunnels, gingerly created side tunnels, or drifts, to be filled with 2.75 million pounds of
dynamite. This was the most hazardous part, for no one knew for certain if the integrity of the tip of the rock had been weakened, if an

undiscovered flaw would give way, or if the end of the effort would be to drown the miners below.

At times, test holes would break through, and the drillers would be showered with starfish and sea slugs before wooden plugs could be hammered into the leaks.

What must those men have thought, working there in the fetid, stale air, so close to the hellish race that had claimed so many lives?

When the shot went off on the morning of April 7, 1958, it was the largest manmade nonnuclear blast in history. Television viewers around the world watched as the swirling surface of the narrows erupted and 400,000 tons of rock shot from the water.

When the smoke cleared and the last of the water stopped falling, an eddy marked the ship-killer rock that had plagued travelers for centuries.

Blasting the top off eliminated the worst of the overfalls and the danger of hitting the rock itself. Yet no one who has seen the tide running at strength has anything less than the most sobering respect for the hazards it still presents.

THE RAPIDS. On a June morning in 1981, vessels of all sorts gathered at Seymour Narrows during the last stages of the flood tide. They waited for slack water, when the current in the passages ahead would be relatively still and it would be safe to proceed. They had left Seattle, or Vancouver, or any one of a dozen other towns together the evening before, but had lost sight of one another in the cross-strait traffic or against the maze of lights on shore. In the pale dawn they found themselves coming together again, their courses converging at Cape Mudge, the entrance to the narrows.

The fleet of waiting vessels began at the Copper Cliffs on the Quadra Island shore, three miles south. In 1898 to 1910 or so, when many ships were going north to the gold rush through these rapids, settlers on shore would hear dogs barking on the ships waiting for the fog to lift or the current to ease. They'd row out and climb aboard, talk, get the news from north and south, until it was time for the ships to proceed.

Today, the waiting craft were different. A diesel tug with a huge barge behind it jogged slowly into the current, keeping station, watching the water pouring out of the gorge ahead and waiting for the slack. The barge carried a year's supply of fuel and provisions for some lonely port in western Alaska, ice-free for a few short months. A couple dozen fish boats waited there, headed for Icy Strait in Southeast Alaska, or Oona River in upper British Columbia, or perhaps the village of Nikolski in the treeless Aleutian Islands. A long, ungainly "floater" (fish-processing ship) was there also, with a large crew, some of them seeing shipboard life for the first time. They were looking out and wondering what all the boats were waiting for.

As the south-flowing flood diminished, boats began to shoot through the gap from the north, leaning hard in the current, first one way, then the other as they struggled to maintain control, before passing quickly by the waiting vessels on the south side and into the strait beyond.

The more powerful of the waiting vessels throttled up, gathered speed against the current, and moved along the shore, trying to stay out of the tidal stream until they were abeam Maude Island. Then they entered the tidal river pouring from the narrows, shouldered their way into midchannel, and disappeared into the gap in the hills.

As the current slowed and the brief period of slack water approached, the floater lumbered away from the shore toward the narrows to resume its long journey north. As it entered the gap, passing beneath the great swoop of the power cables, the crew looked back at the smoke and the stacks of the mills at Campbell River, watching the little yard tugs towing log rafts from the booming ground behind Defender Shoal in Menzies Bay.

Ahead, past North Bluff, Puget Bluff, Plumper Point, and Separation Head, lay a very different world, the land and the waterways wilder, lonelier. The highway near the shore would become a logging road on the hillside, the frieze of houses and towns on the water giving way to small settlements with greater and greater distances between them. The very air drawing down the gorge from Johnstone Strait would become raw and cool.

No northbound mariner may pass from the Strait of Georgia to the lonelier land beyond without going through one of the several narrow passes or rapids. It is as if along each route nature set an obstacle before the traveler, a sobering barrier placed to warn of what lay beyond.

Just before 8:00 P.M. on May 30, 1972, I approached Yuculta Rapids, Alaska-bound at last in my own boat, a 32-foot salmon gill-netter.

The longest day of the year was three weeks away and the northern sun was high in the sky. We jogged in the heavy current swirls by Whirlpool Point, getting our bearings; both the pilot book and experienced friends had spoken of the need for caution there. The chart bore this notation in red letters: "CAUTION—Violent eddies and whirlpools form in Devils Hole." The fish stand on Stuart Island, marked as "conspicuous" on the chart, was gone, but the whirlpools, marked as black swirls, were definitely there.

> "Slack . . . in the Yucultas? Nosir, no *sir*, don't be expecting no slack in *that* place. You get all that water up in Bute Inlet, see, especially it's been raining inland, and it's too much for 'er, she just comes pouring out of there one way, and pow, she just turns around and runs hard the other way, she jes ain't got no *time* for slack, see now?"
>
> —A local resident

I had seen whirlpools, both from the shore and from the two-story pilothouse of a 90-footer in Seymour seven years before. But on that day, from our little boat, just a few feet above the water, it was very, very different.

They were much bigger than I remembered, some almost a hundred yards across, their centers sinking to dark holes with shining sides that disappeared below my line of sight. But it was the speed at which they revolved that was so sobering, and I felt my throat go dry, my heart begin to pound. Furthermore, in addition to spinning, the whirlpools were also moving rapidly across the channel, pushed by the current. Sometimes there would be three or four great spinning pools, revolving slowly around each other, filling up almost the entire bay between Whirlpool Point and Jimmy Judd Island.

This was the place where the natives said even whales waited for slack. They'd see them from the shore, swimming ponderously back and forth outside the rapids, blowing and diving, then all pushing through together when the current eased. And it was here that Vancouver's men had had to pull their boats through with lines from the shore, helped by the natives.

We'd been warned of tugs towing ungainly log rafts, and I looked enviously to the west toward narrow Innes Passage as maybe a safer way through. But the Hydrographic Service's *Sailing Directions* calls that a bad idea, remarking on the need for "intimate local knowledge" to traverse Innes safely; of that we had none.

By then it was obvious that whatever slack there was had passed and, furthermore, that it was no place to linger, for the current was quickly growing stronger. Picking our path carefully between the whirlpools, we pushed upstream into Guillard Passage and out toward Dent Rapids and Devils Hole, which was marked on the chart with both the black swirls *and* the wavy lines that meant rapids and overfalls. Oh boy.

The current seemed to run a little less hard by the shore, so we traveled along the edge of the kelp, watching out for fast-moving whirlpools that might shove us into the beach. When we were through the worst of it I looked back. There was a marked vee of smooth water in the middle of Dent Rapids, as in a swiftly flowing river, before the water tumbled and boiled in the eddies beyond.

Just north of the rapids the chart had a warning in red letters: "CAUTION—A dangerous whirlpool forms over the 3.3 shoal on large tides," but before I could figure out what a large tide was, we were past.

By Horn Point, a little way north of the rapids, we could breathe easier, and I got a chance to look around. The sun that had beat down so warmly a half hour earlier was behind the dark shoulder of Mount Tucker on Sonora Island, and the air was suddenly cool. Gone was the cheering sight of the fishing resorts at Big Bay and Stuart Island, their skiffs trolling along the fringes of the current for tyees or springs, the Canadian terms for king salmon.

WATCH OUT FOR KELP! Along most of the British Columbia coast, kelp grows on rocks close to the surface during the summer and fall. By staying away from kelp, a vessel can generally stay clear of danger. Vessels should be wary of approaching kelp when the current is running, as the fronds will stream away

Salmon boats **Restless** *and* **Merry Maid** *negotiate the sheltered inside waters of Cordero Channel.*

from the rock, and not necessarily be directly over it. As the trusty government pilot book says, "It should be an invariable rule never to pass over kelp."

—Notebook

We traveled on a ribbon of water at the bottom of a steep and thickly forested fjord. Only the quick-flashing red light at the entrance to the rapids behind us showed that man had, indeed, ever passed that way.

A thin layer of clouds replaced the pale blue of the sky, and even inside the cozy cabin of our boat with the smell of supper cooking on the stove, I shivered, unexpectedly. At the bright fair day, so suddenly gone gray and cool. At the once-friendly shore so quickly turned somber, threatening.

Fifteen minutes later we came to a place where two narrow canyons, Nodales Channel and Frederick Arm, branched to starboard and to port. Seen in the flat evening light, they looked alike, each a steep-sided gorge, the passage quickly lost from sight around a bend in the channel.

Susanna and I spoke little for the next few minutes, awed and sobered by such a change in the landscape and the mood in just a few miles. Our northern journey, so pleasant up to then, with sunny stopovers and easy runs in between, was now revealed as something quite different. When we rounded a point a few miles later and entered Shoal Bay, it was with relief that we saw another boat's lights, friendly beacons in the vast and rapidly darkening country that stretched away on all sides.

While the Yuculta route, via Calm, Cordero, Chancellor, Wellbore and Sunderland channels and thence into Johnstone Strait, is sheltered, one must still contend with Whirlpool and Greene Point rapids as well. Although less dangerous than the Yucultas, these two tidal narrows constrict the channel enough that passage against the current is difficult except for powerful vessels. Many vessels try to traverse the three rapids in a single tide. To do this and catch slack water at the worst of the three—Yuculta Rapids—generally means running the other two with a considerable current. Vessels will occasionally underestimate the time needed to accomplish this and arrive at the Yucultas after slack, which is bad.

"When we were still two miles away from the upper rapids, I could feel the boat start to speed up. But before I really had time to consider whether we should wait until the next slack, the current had a hold of us and we were shoved ahead, through the upper rapids and into the whirlpools on the other side. The worst of it was that you couldn't really slow down, for each time we tried, the scow we were towing would charge ahead, or sheer violently off to one side.

"Once that current had a hold on us, we got sucked through the first rapids and then we were into the worst of the bunch: the Yucultas.

"Before I could really formulate any strategy other than *keep the tow line tight!*, lest it be swept under our stern and into our propeller, the tidal stream had sucked us into the gap, and quickly downhill. We shot from between the islands, took a violent lurch to starboard, and entered a great whirlpool. We were all up on the flying bridge, and as we watched in horror, the scow we were towing sheered way out, barely clearing a reef, until it was *passing* us, the tow line going completely slack! I tried to speed up and take up the slack, but then the tow took another violent sheer the *other* way, and then, with both of us traveling in opposite directions, the tow line came tight so suddenly that it almost pulled the scow sideways and under water before she came around. If it hadn't been for the tire that we had rigged as a shock absorber, the line would have parted.

"We entered another whirlpool, started to spin totally around, in the grip of the huge rotating mass of water. It was all I could do to keep us ahead of the scow we were towing, but it was over as quick as it had begun; the tide pushed us out of the rapids, the channel widened, I stopped our engine, and we lay for a long time, just drifting in the current, watching the rest of our traveling companions struggle through the white water behind. One by one, like rafts or kayaks finishing up a run down through a stretch of white water, they shot through the gap and twisted and turned through the whirlpools and eddies before finally making the smooth water beyond."

—A friend

He was towing a small scow, or barge. Compared to a raft of logs, a scow is easy to tow. A log raft consists of hundreds of bundles of logs, constrained into a roughly rectangular shape by perimeter logs chained together. Imagine trying to tow such a thing, or, as is usually the case, several of them hooked together, through these passes and rapids, where slack water sometimes lasts but a few minutes.

Today, much of the long-distance log transport from the immense forests of northern British Columbia and the Queen Charlotte Islands is conducted by self-dumping barges. The logs are loaded on top of the barges and towed rapidly to their destinations, where, with the opening of valves to ballast tanks, the barges are made to lean over until the wood slides off.

But much of the wood cut in lower British Columbia still travels through these constricted channels in big, wide, log rafts, which even the most powerful tug can barely tow at more than a walking pace. They rafts are also hard to see, especially at night.

Towing logs is slow work, and weather and boredom aren't the only hazard. In 1914, the skipper of the tug *Warrior,* towing a couple of big log booms, or rafts, looked back in amazement as his raft bulged upward in the middle as if hung up on a rock, though he *knew* he was in deep water. The bulge turned out to be the Chilean submarine, *Iquique*, surfacing under his logs. The raft had to be dismantled to free the sub.

Reading towboat lights—The mariner should be on constant alert at night for tugs towing long tows, whose lights may or may not be visible. Tugs with a tow more than six hundred feet astern are required to show three white lights in a vertical line on the mast, visible through 360 degrees. Any mariner encountering a vessel lit in such a fashion should assume that it is towing one or more barges or rafts, and make every effort to determine the length and position of the tows, before attempting to pass or cross the course of the tow.

Especially hazardous to navigation are log rafts, which frequently are marked only by kerosene lamps displayed at the corner of the raft or boom. It is not uncommon to have these lights so obscured by soot as to be almost invisible. Furthermore, the logs, riding but a few feet out of the water at best, are almost impossible to see until a vessel is almost on top of them.

Perhaps the worst scenario is for a small vessel to pass at night or in poor visibility between a tug and a barge. The tow line will be submerged behind the tug, and the small vessel may not even realize the hazard until the barge looms out of the night, traveling at perhaps 15-20 knots, and easily able to trample a small vessel beneath its wide, sloping bow.   —Notebook

JOHNSTONE STRAIT.   No matter how northbound vessels travel, whether through Seymour Narrows, the Yucultas, or the even-narrower passages available, sooner or later they have to face Johnstone Strait.

It is a windy place. The tide runs hard. There are few anchorages. For sixty miles there is only the long shoulder of Vancouver Island on the south and the dark forested shores of upcoast British Columbia on the north. The scenery, especially in the spring and fall when snow lies on the hills, is grand. Yet, there is something about the scale of things here—the width of the channel, the panorama of hill line after hill line without settlement or building—that makes one, especially in smaller craft, uneasy, yearning for narrower channels, cozier harbors.

In the summer especially, when the land masses to the east and south warm up, a westerly breeze rises at midday to boom down the

While larger salmon trollers often fish thirty to forty miles from shore and anchor on the "grounds" at night, smaller boats such as these fish closer to shore and spend evenings anchored in quiet bays.

strait until after dark. When opposed by an ebbing tide, it makes short, steep seas through which travel is awkward. Where the strait narrows or where channels enter from the north, confused currents make conditions worse. As an early pilot book put it, "We advise all good sailors to travel Johnstone Strait between dawn and noon, and not linger."

In October 1975 at Growler Cove, Johnstone Strait showed us one of its many faces.

We arrived in the late afternoon, and as we tied our 50-foot fish boat to a broken and half-sunk float, the sun line of the Vancouver Island hills rose higher and higher on the mountains of West Cracroft and Harbledown islands, the low, slanting light making the air itself shine.

I stepped out after supper and walked to the far side of the float. The air had grown cold, and my footprints were dark on the newly frosted wood. Above us, the stars shone coldly on the snowy hills and the strait that lay like a great still canyon before us. Before going to bed, I looked out again. Out in the strait, the tide had begun to run, the rushing waters echoing hollowly, distinctly, and far away.

In the morning when we awoke, a heavier snow had come to the hills, yet not to the shore. All around us, the land, starting at about a thousand feet up, was white, and on it the sun, rising finally from a nameless peak in the wild land to the east, shone suddenly with a brilliant yellow light.

We returned many times. In October 1982, after a windy passage from the north, Mary Lou and I anchored our big fish packer in nearby Blenkinsop Bay, uninhabited, but a refuge from the windy strait outside.

Sometime after midnight, I awoke and went out on deck. The wind had stopped. The night was very still. The stars were lost behind thick clouds, and our masthead anchor light had burned out. The only spot of light anywhere was inside, where the flame in the galley stove danced behind a sooty mica oval. I felt my way over to the rail and stopped for a moment, then moved back to sit on the hatch, uneasy at the complete absence of light outside. For when I'd stood at the rail, it was so totally silent and black that instead of water below, I imagined only a void, into which a stone, dropped, would fall soundlessly, forever.

Of the natives, the settlers, the loggers, and the fishermen that once inhabited the myriad inlets and islands that lay to the north, there was little sign.

Yet this stretch of the coast was home to the Kwakiutl Indians. Before logging and fishing became highly capitalized and centralized operations, it was alive with settlers and hopeful entrepreneurs as well. Wherever there were a few acres of meadow, there might be a farm family selling their produce to the loggers and fishermen. Wherever there was a steep patch of good timber, a hand logger might be at work, sliding his trees into the water, making up a raft for a tug to take to the mills.

POTLATCH. A native tradition that puzzled whites was the potlatch, which was used to celebrate an event, such as an important person's marriage, someone's elevation to chief, and so on. The key feature of the celebration, a party that often went on for days, was the host's giving gifts to the guests. The value and number of gifts showed the wealth and power of the host. Within time, the favor was returned.

After the first trading posts were established in the 1840s and 1850s and European goods became available, the bigger potlatches became transfers of wealth. To put on a memorable potlatch, a chief might give away most of his wealth and possessions.

Missionaries and people in the provincial government who were finding themselves extending increasing services to the Indians didn't understand why so much wealth was being given away in potlatches. The facts that the wealth was really being passed back and forth and that the potlatch was a traditional cornerstone of Pacific Northwest Coast native culture weren't truly comprehended by the government, and potlatches were outlawed beginning in the 1880s.

This was easier said than done. The natives moved the potlatches to more remote spots and tried to celebrate them without the knowledge of the provincial authorities.

In December of 1921, the Kwakiutl from Alert Bay began slipping away to Village Island. The occasion was Chief Dan Cranmer's famous Christmas Tree Potlatch. He invited three or four hundred guests from as far away as Smith Inlet, and gave away enough stuff to supply a good-sized village for a winter: twenty-four canoes, four gas boats, four hundred Hudson's Bay blankets, a thousand tin washbasins, a thousand sacks of flour, sewing machines, and so on.

A zealous Indian Agent arrested the chief along with 21 other natives. They were convicted and sent to prison. Most of the gifts were confiscated and sat in a warehouse for decades. Potlatching continued to be carried out in secret but the institution became weakened.

In 1951, the anti-potlatching laws were repealed, and eventually the stolen articles were returned to the natives, providing the basis for what is now the Cape Mudge Museum on Quadra Island and the U'Mista Cultural Center at Alert Bay. By then, fifty years later, things had come full circle. After causing significant damage to many aspects of Pacific Northwest Coast society, the provincial authorities O.K.'d potlatches again, in hopes of their becoming tourist attractions.

～～～

FLOATING HOMES. Many of the first settlements in the steep coun-try north of Seymour Narrows were groups of floating homes, built on rafts of cedar, spruce, or fir logs cabled together. House rafts were tied one to another to make little communities in bays and inlets too rugged for building on shore. They were whole little neighborhoods, where chickens wandered across the logs, gardens grew in boxes and barrels, and children crossed the logs to a floating school. When the fishing played out or the logs became too difficult to harvest, the whole town would move on, towed to a more promising spot.

That is, if they could find a tug willing to do the job. Tug captains were reluctant to tow floating towns any distance. To lose a raft of logs when the wind came up was one thing, but to have a whole town go ashore and break up on the rocks was another.

Hospitals floated. The Texada Island hospital, once a floating dance hall, was towed to another location when the mines on Texada closed. On its way to a third location years later, the hospital was caught out in a gale in Johnstone Strait, and it blew ashore and broke up.

Around the turn of the century, the Newfoundland-born master mariner and Anglican minister, John Antle, while rowing and sailing his 14-foot skiff from Vancouver to Alert Bay (220 miles), realized the need for medical and religious services along the coast. He persuaded his church to help start several hospitals and to fit out a small hospital ship, the *Columbia*.

One had to be creative to transport injured and sick people to help. Once when Antle found a sick woman with no one to care for her children, he towed her whole house to the nearest place with medical facilities.

At times, church services were cut short when a medical emergency arose.

Once when [John Antle] was conducting a service in the chapel of the *Columbia*, a man shouted from the shore that there had been a bad accident in a camp up Johnstone Strait. Antle slammed closed the Bible, pulled off his surplice, started the motor, cast off and headed out. One of the abandoned worshipers, hastily leaping ashore, remarked, "That was the best sermon I ever heard!"

—Beth Hill, *Upcoast Summers*

Life wasn't easy for the settlers. Few had motorized vessels; many rowed great distances in small boats to take out produce or bring in supplies. John Manson of Cortes Island rowed a hundred miles to the head of Knight Inlet and back again, bringing two school-age girls to his home so that, with his own children, he'd qualify for a state-supplied teacher. When Ernest Halliday and his brother William arrived, rowing and sailing, at the head of Kingcome Inlet to carve a ranch out of the wilderness in 1893, they were sixty miles from Alert Bay, the nearest settlement. Nevertheless, when they had beef to sell, they rowed it to market, two days there and two days back.

For a time, in the first quarter of this century, enough of an economy existed along Johnstone Strait to support steamships, which would stop at the settlements, take produce to market, and bring in supplies. The weekly stop of the Union Steamship boat was an occasion when rowboats and little gas putt-putts would come from the farthest nooks, the most isolated inlets, to get mail or supplies and to drop off or pick up passengers.

But logging became more centralized even before the Depression, as did fishing. One by one, many of the settlements visited by early travelers disappeared; the homesteaders moved to more populated areas, and the woods closed in around the ruins.

In the region northwest of the Yucultas, the mainland shore is deeply indented with long winding fjords and is separated from Johnstone Strait by a complex maze of islands as well.

> Connected to the [Johnstone] strait are several extensive inlets, the shores of which rise in almost sheer precipices to stupendous peaks, clad in perpetual snow. The inlets are very dreary and gloomy, due to their being overshadowed by the heights of the mountains and to the frequent mist and rain.
>
> —*Sailing Directions*

Knight and the other inlets in the region are for the most part so *steep-to*, meaning the deep water extends right up to the shore, that anchoring is difficult. In Wahshihlas Bay, for example, *Sailing Directions* suggests a vessel may anchor in 25 fathoms (150 feet deep) with its stern tied to a tree on shore.

Yesterday, we had passed a slender Indian dugout. An Indian was standing up in the bow, holding aloft a long fish-spear poised, ready to strike. His woman was crouched in the stern, balancing the canoe with her paddle—a high sheer cliff behind them. Cliff, dugout, primitive man; all were mirrored in the still water beneath them. He struck—tossed the wriggling fish into the dugout, and resumed his pose. When was it that we had watched them? Yesterday? a hundred years ago? or just somewhere on that curve of time?

Farther and farther into that past we slipped. Down winding tortuous byways—strewn with reefs, fringed with kelp. Now and then, out of pity for our propeller, we poled our way through the cool, green shallows—slipping over the pointed groups of great starfish, all purple and red and blue, turning aside the rock cod swimming with their lazy tails; making the minnows wheel and dart among the sea grapes.

—M. Wylie Blanchet, *The Curve of Time*

The writer was a widow, Muriel Blanchet, traveling in a 25-foot boat with her five children in the 1930s to explore the intricate waterways on the east side of Johnstone Strait. Her book, *The Curve of Time*, is an unaffected and powerful account of her travels to remote and abandoned native villages in a time when yachts were few. Through her eyes one sees the coast at a time when many of the big Kwakiutl villages were still occupied. Wherever this remarkable woman and her tribe of children saw white shell mounds, or middens, they stopped and explored them, finding abandoned villages where the Kwakiutl spirits seemed to linger still.

People-who-live-in-big-houses was how the natives of the interior referred to the coastal people, for their habit of building and living in great long lodges, several families to a structure. Although many are rotted and fallen now, the great houses were lived in and maintained until a few decades ago.

We dropped anchor between a small island and a great rugged cliff topped with moss-laden firs that bounded one end of the beach. Then we piled into the dinghy and rowed ashore. The place was deserted, for it is a winter village, and every summer the tribe goes off for the fishing. So, when we landed, no chief came down with greetings, no one sang the song of welcome, only a great black wooden figure, standing waist high in the nettles up on the bank, welcomed us with outstretched arms.

"Is she calling us?" asked John, anxiously, shrinking closer to me.

I looked at the huge figure with the fallen breasts, the pursed-out lips, the greedy arms. It was Dsonoqua, of Indian folklore, who runs whistling through the woods, calling to the little Indian children so that she can catch them and carry them off in her basket to devour them.

"No, no! Not us!," I assured him. But he kept a watchful eye on her until he was well out of grabbing distance.

Behind the black woman, high up on the midden, sprawled thirteen or fourteen of the old community houses. The same houses stood there when Cook and Vancouver visited the coast. When Columbus discovered America, another group of buildings stood on the same site, only the midden was lower.

—Blanchet, *The Curve of Time*

Today the forest has swallowed many of the villages, the totems, the great lodges, and the intricate ceremonial carvings. Until relatively recently, however, travelers in the more remote stretches of the coast were apt to encounter villages with the lodges intact, although the inhabitants were gone. Visitors would encounter the eerie sight of the dead, boxed and placed among the limbs of huge old cedars or firs at a special burial site.

In time, the government forbade tree burial, and the long arm of Canadian provincial law reached even the remoter sections of the coast. After this, native families, or "crests," of the coast would pick a little island near the village for a burying place, putting the dead in boxes in small log shelters. Each island might be marked with a sign on which was painted the pictograph or symbol of that family.

Mrs. Blanchet found such a sign near Knight Inlet. Made of wood and perhaps thirty feet long, the sign depicted a wolf running. On a nearby islet was another pictograph, that of a killer whale.

Though today's traveler wouldn't find native villages as Muriel Blanchet did in the 1930s, much of this country, especially the remote inlets, is the way it was in Vancouver's time: wild and empty.

QUEEN CHARLOTTE STRAIT.   At the western end of these water-ways is a place where conversation stops. Whoever is on board and not steering comes up into the pilothouse, or, in a smaller boat, just up to the front, to stand by the windows, to look ahead, to see what it will be like "out there."

The place is Pulteney Point, and it marks the beginning of wide waters: Queen Charlotte Strait. For vessels traveling sheltered routes, this is the most open water seen so far, and it gives a glimpse of what lies ahead: Queen Charlotte Sound, the crossing of which can be the worst part of any trip up or down the Inside Passage. Beyond Pulteney Point, the strait widens to fifteen miles across. The lower shores of the far side are hidden from sight by the curve of the earth.

The Vancouver Island shore along here is low and undistinguished, the anchorages indifferent. The land seems unfriendly, the miles to pass, slower. For small craft northbound, the next destination is twenty-two miles past Pulteney Point, a little cove on Hurst Island travelers have come to call God's Pocket.

These twenty-two miles can be long and nasty. If the weather turns vicious, one can duck into Beaver Harbour, on the southern shore of which is the native village of Fort Rupert. Here in 1849 the Hudson's Bay Company built the fort and store, and the first great potlatch cele-brations were held by the tribes using the newly available European goods as gifts.

This is the northern end of Vancouver Island, a gloomy and somber place. No longer does the high mountain backbone of the island deflect the North Pacific gales, and the land shows it. The islands here are steep, hard, and mean-looking, their shores guarded by breaking reefs and ledges, the trees bent and twisted by the wind. One has a very clear sense of the wild and rough land and seas that lie to the west.

At Triangle Island, off the western tip of Vancouver Island, a light-house was built on top of a 600-foot cliff. The buildings had to be guyed with heavy wires, lest they be blown away. Even so, a storm blew the radio towers away and moved the office off its concrete foundation and shoved it against the generator building. Only that building's full water tanks saved it and the office from following the radio towers over the cliff. Another breeze blew the doors and windows and most of the roof off the bunkhouse, and the crew's clothes and bedding out into space. It wasn't a popular duty spot for lighthouse crews, who were sometimes told they were just going for a few weeks, only to be left there for a year. In November 1918, the lighthouse tender *Galiano* stopped there briefly to drop off supplies. A gale was approaching. She and her twenty-six people disappeared in the storm. Shortly thereafter, the lighthouse was abandoned.

GOD'S POCKET.   The harbor at God's Pocket: in more sheltered waters, mariners wouldn't give such a small and relatively open cove a second look when seeking an anchorage. A surge comes in from any swell in the Sound, and there isn't room for but a handful of boats. One sleeps uneasily; even though the wind doesn't reach down to the cove, it rushes through the trees above.

Yet what shelter it offers lies at the very edge of Queen Charlotte Sound. By lying here, a northbound vessel may make a 3:00 or 4:00 A.M. start and perhaps get across the open waters to the north before the wind starts to blow. Likewise, southbound travelers, arriving here at dark after a difficult passage, find the limited shelter infinitely better than what they came from.

One year just before Halloween, we came here after crossing Queen Charlotte Sound in a rapidly worsening southerly gale. Our steering failed as we entered the cove. After all we'd been through, I only wanted to anchor and rest. But the cove was full; there was no room for us. We managed to tie to another anchored boat for a few minutes while we repaired the steering. Then we steamed around to Browning Passage, two miles west, to try to get the anchor to hold in the narrow gut between Balaklava Island and the Lucan Islands. We snuggled in as close to the trees as we dared and the anchor grabbed on the third try. It wasn't much of a berth. Although we were sheltered from the seas, the wind eddied violently through the gorge, slamming into us, shaking the rigging with its fury.

As we cleaned away the stuff that had broken loose during the crossing and dug out the rum, we made out the lights of several vessels, bucking heavily into the seas as they worked their way into the anchorage from Queen Charlotte Sound. When they passed in close by to anchor ahead of us, we noticed a broken-out pilothouse window on one, snapped off antennas and rigging on the other.

The night came on early, impenetrable, filled with wind and rain. The surf and the foghorn at Scarlett Point, a mile and a half away, carried clearly to us through the trees.

Again and again, a heavy gust slammed violently into us. I got up, looked out, turned on the spotlight, and made sure the anchor wasn't dragging. The trees and shore, two boat lengths away, were lost in the slashing rain, and only the bar-tight anchor wire told me we were still holding.

Deep in the night, I awoke and listened to an odd, hollow, scraping sound. I lay in my bunk wondering what it might be, when WHAM, a 45-foot wooden troller slammed into me, the sound being his anchor cable scraping along mine, and I stumbled up and out into the roaring night to help him get clear.

Still, with the wind howling in the rigging, the seas breaking heavily on the outside shores, and the foghorn shaking the wild night all around us, we savored that scant shelter as a yachtsman might a berth in the best marina.

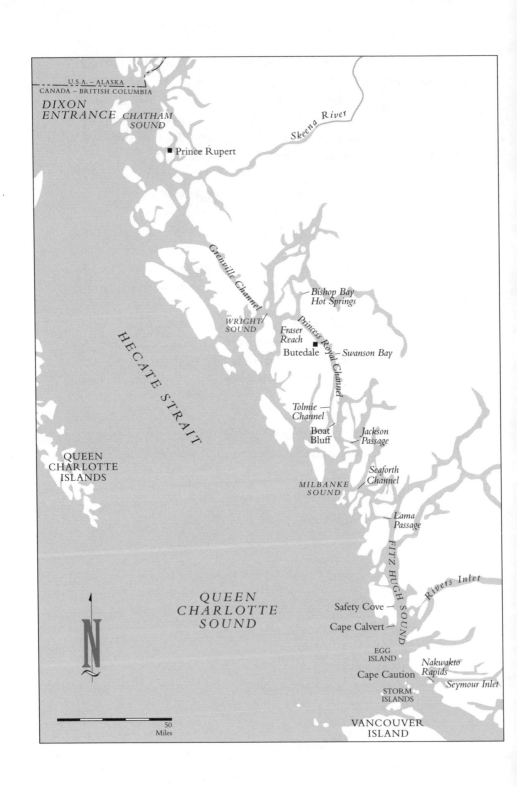

U.S.A. – ALASKA
CANADA – BRITISH COLUMBIA

DIXON
ENTRANCE CHATHAM
SOUND

Skeena River

■ Prince Rupert

Grenville Channel

WRIGHT
SOUND

Bishop Bay
Hot Springs

Princess Royal Channel

Fraser
Reach
Butedale ■
Swanson Bay

HECATE STRAIT

Tolmie
Channel

Boat
Bluff

Jackson
Passage

Seaforth
Channel

QUEEN
CHARLOTTE
ISLANDS

MILBANKE
SOUND

Lama
Passage

FITZ HUGH SOUND

Rivers Inlet

QUEEN
CHARLOTTE
SOUND

Safety Cove

Cape Calvert

N

EGG
ISLAND

Nakwakto
Rapids

Cape Caution

Seymour Inlet

STORM
ISLANDS

50
Miles

VANCOUVER
ISLAND

CHAPTER THREE

The Northern Canyons

QUEEN CHARLOTTE SOUND
TO CHATHAM SOUND

"**YEAH, THAT WAS '62,** I think. We were on the old *Urania* headed up north with a load of produce. Running vegetables, hams, apples, spuds, whatever the skipper thought he could turn a buck on, that was kind of our winter fishery back then. We'd load up in Seattle and head up to Southeast and go from town to town, selling. In the beginning, we'd take a newspaper or radio ad, but after a few trips, just as soon as we tied up at the dock, the word would get around that the vegetable boat was in, and people would start coming down. 'Course the local storekeepers didn't think too much of our operation. Our stuff was fresher and cheaper than theirs. So what could they do?

"Anyway, the old *Urania,* she was narrow, see, and wouldn't she roll when she got out into it! That trip was mid-December, and we had her loaded with all she could carry and then some. Man, there were spuds in the hold, apples in the lazarette, carrots on the flying bridge, all the spare bunks down in the fo'c's'le filled up with hams, and then we musta' had two, three hundred squashes jammed in up around the bow and anchor winch.

"'Course, running with produce and all, you don't want to stop unless you really have to: the sooner you get there the fresher it is and all, so usually we'd just run through, weather or not.

"You could tell soon as we left Scarlett Point that we were in for something. It was one of those afternoons that just smelled like a weather breeder: big, oily swell and a queer-looking sky to the north. Well, the skipper just headed out, and we crossed our fingers and didn't say nothin'.

"I want to tell you, she come on some quick at Storm Islands. That first gust musta' been fifty, sixty right on the nose, getting worse all the time, blowing the tops off all the swells. I figured we'd be lucky to get across in one piece, it come on that bad. And of course, we started dipping our bow, and there went the squashes, spilling out over the bow and out over the goddamn Sound.

"Then the skipper slows down and starts yelling to start picking up the goddamn squashes out of the water, fer crissake. I waved to him to keep going, to get the hell across before it got any worse, but he kept pointing to the squashes bobbing up and down in them seas.

"By then it must have been gusting seventy, easy, and that old slab of a boat was damn near rolling rails under in them seas, but the old man had to get all them squashes and that was all there was to it. So there we were, chasing around the whole ocean, trying to corral all them fewking squashes with a dip net."

—A friend

A fisherman in a small fishing boat had it no easier:

"Five days we'd waited in Safety Cove that fall. We ran out of food, but luckily a big tug was laying in there and sold us some steaks and bread. But then we ran out of diapers and I sure as heck wasn't going to be stuck in that little 32-footer with no diapers for two kids, so we *had* to get out of there. On the sixth day it stopped blowing just around dark, with another gale supposed to hit the next day. So it was go in the black or wait for who the hell knows how long for another chance.

"Then we got out into it, and God, you wouldn't have believed the swells. Fifteen years I've been going up and down the coast, spring, summer, and fall, and I've never seen 'em like that—no wind, but these huge monster swells—some must have been thirty feet at least. And the logs—it was just after some huge tides, and they must have picked stuff off the beaches that had been there for years—big logs and whole trees. We had to have the spotlight on the whole way across. It was like there was a whole forest in the water that you had to try and pick your way through. That was five years ago, and still, sometimes I come awake in the middle of the night, and I'm right there all over again, the spotlight showing each swell totally full of wood. It was a nightmare."

—A friend

A passenger vessel almost 300 feet long was battered:

"It was three years ago, in January. I think we were on the *Malaspina* that trip, or maybe the *Taku* [Alaska state ferries]. I can't remember which boat we were on, but it was Queen Charlotte, I'm sure of that.

"We came across just at dark. It was blowing hard northwest, and even on the slow bell, we were bucking pretty hard. A lot of the passengers were in their cabins laying low, but I went up forward, into the forward salon where you can just like sit in some easy chairs and look out forward. I remember we had just passed Cape Caution when it started to come on bad. Even on the slow bell, we'd dip the bow on the big ones, and that's on a ship almost three hundred feet long.

"Then something broke loose down below [on the vehicle deck]; the crew told me later it was a big truck that started it. I guess all that bucking must have loosened the chains, until it got some slack, and finally popped 'em.

"Mister, I want to tell you, that was some noise. First it was just the truck smashing back and forth, but then it busted some other big trailers loose o' their chains, and they started smashing against God knows how many campers and pickups, and you could hear the dogs barking, but they couldn't let anyone get out onto the car deck the way things were sliding and crashing. I was worried about the gasoline more than anything else.

"The worst of it was that they couldn't do anything. The tide was starting to run and the wind was coming on some more, so they had to just keep going until they got up under the land, in by [Cape] Calvert . . . at Ketchikan they had to pull half a dozen rigs out of there with the tow truck . . . they was just wrecks."

—A friend

Cape Caution, Storm Islands, Safety Cove, God's Pocket. Such are the way points along this route. The names tell the story.

Almost everyone who has spent time on the northern coast has a story about crossing Queen Charlotte Sound. There is no inside route here, just forty miles of open water. Even vessels taking a more easterly route along the deeply indented mainland coast face runs along rugged shores exposed to the swells and seas of the Sound.

The gold-hungry men bound for the Klondike diggings had to cross here, as did most of the pioneers who settled Alaska and upcoast British Columbia. What might they have thought of the land where they were headed as they peered out from the crowded, creaking hulls of tired steamers, seeing the seas pound those lonely shores?

In my 1975 logbook, the entry for October 27 is a scrawl, as if I had been busy with other things:

"1230 Egg Island, sloppy, SE 20.

"1320 Cape Caution, SE 25, four-foot chop, wet going.

"1600 Pine Island, gale warning, wind here 40–45 SE, very shitty going, had to tack down around Pine Island."

Our boat that year was a ferrocement 50-footer (a hull made of concrete and steel). This one had a bad habit of filling her lazarette, or stern compartment, in a following sea. The hold was filled with heavy Seattle-bound freight, so we were traveling uncomfortably deep in the water. Should the lazarette fill, the vessel would sink like the stone she was.

The weather report had been good when we entered the Sound, but a long dark line lay on the southern horizon.

Rough seas make for dusty going in Queen Charlotte Sound.

At Egg Island the wind came. In that country, at that time of year, the storms euphemistically called "Pacific disturbances" can last for days. One such storm washed most of the buildings that housed the light-keeper at Egg Island into the sea. The lightkeeper and his wife survived, but they never wanted a lighthouse job again.

I suppose the prudent mariner would have turned around when the wind started. Yet, in the fall, along the north coast of British Columbia, such a strategy might also mean never getting where you are going.

At Cape Caution, the tide was flowing against the wind, steepening the seas and shortening the distance between them. On occasion, our heavily laden boat could not rise quickly enough, and green water came over the high bow; I was concerned that a wave larger than the rest would break out a pilothouse window. I looked around, seeking the comfort of the sight of another vessel. But there was only the dark, inhospitable shore and the white-streaked ocean. I wanted badly to turn around. There were emergency harbors downwind of us at Miles Inlet to the east and Millbrook Cove to the north. Yet I knew neither place. The season was late, the light would go quickly, and the idea of approaching them before a heavy gale in failing light with no radar had little appeal. By then we were more than halfway across, past that invisible point at which it was better to go on than to turn around.

Also, I just wanted to get across. If it was going to blow for a week, I knew that probably I could still sneak along the shore of Vancouver Island, once I'd made it to God's Pocket.

At Storm Islands it was terrible. It wasn't so much the wind, but the tide pushing hard against it, making for a confused mess in which the seas came from every direction. We found a patch of sheltered water about the size of a house lot, but only by approaching dangerously close to the rocky shore. We stopped for a few minutes, just idling into wind and sea while I checked the skiff, the lazarette, the bilge, the engine, before we put our nose out into it for the next lap. The radio told us what we already knew: there was a gale in Queen Charlotte. The next hour was agony. The boat began to feel logy, heavy; I feared the lazarette was filling, and I couldn't tell if its little electric bilge pump was gaining or losing, yet I didn't dare leave the wheel. Even if I were able to get back to the stern to check, I was afraid to take the hatch covers off for fear a sea would sweep over and fill us.

Our course for the leg to Pine Island was at right angles to the storm. We tried it briefly, and the seas rolled across our deck. So we tacked, quartering down away from the seas for a mile or so and then quartering up into them, almost doubling the distance we had to travel.

At Pine Island it was almost dark. Some of the gusts were over sixty, tearing the tops off the waves and flinging them far downwind and turning the whole Sound white.

The island is a few hundred acres of cliff, rock, and wind-twisted trees, but there was a lighthouse there and, best of all, the cozy and brightly lit lightkeeper's house. Oh, how the sight cheered us that wild and stormy afternoon. The storm boiled and raged in white foaming seas past the point. I wanted to stay, to jog for the night below the friendly, lighted windows. To lie there seemed immeasurably better than heading out into the gale again, almost surely to be overtaken by darkness before we could make shelter.

But I knew that in October gale warnings can become storm warnings, and that in similar conditions a 160-footer in Hecate Strait to the north had had her deck cargo of aluminum skiffs twisted and broken by the seas, surviving only through good fortune. We pumped the lazarette dry, checked the whole vessel over, and set out.

In my logbook that night, after we'd finally made the shelter of the land, in the very last column, past "wind," "tide," and "barometer," is "weather and remarks." It's only a small space, but what powerful feelings are hidden in this: "Glad to be inside!"

Imagine what tugs faced as they towed logs across these waters. The big steam and diesel tugs sometimes waited for two weeks or more for weather to make the crossing. Tugs southbound with log tows waited in the Southgate Group, a cluster of islands on the north side of Queen Charlotte Strait. The cliffs and caves around the harbors speak silently of generations of bored tow-boaters: names, dates, even paintings of tugs are on the rock walls.

LOG RAFTS.   Queen Charlotte Sound, or "The Queen's Pond" as it is sometimes called, was too rough for the familiar flat log raft, and so the Davis Raft was developed.

In the 1890s, Oregon loggers and mill owners had tried to move logs to the booming California market in huge ocean-going rafts. It didn't work out. The first one, called a Joggins Raft, was constructed in a cradle in Coos Bay, Oregon. The work took three months, and the product was a cigar-shaped monster almost 500 feet long, the top twenty feet out of the water, all held together with sixty tons of iron chains and complete with a cone-shaped steel nose or bow. It held five million board feet of lumber. The shipping companies, who were making a nice business of transporting the logs and lumber in schooners and steamers to California, a couple hundred thousand board feet at a whack, were unenthusiastic. They needn't have worried.

The first tug to try the ungainly raft was the *Ranger*, an early ocean tug on which the helmsman steered from an unprotected wheel aft on the top deck. (Long on fresh air and visibility but short on protection, this steering arrangement lost favor after breakers on the Columbia River bar cleaned both the steering wheel and the helmsman off one unfortunate tug.)

The *Ranger* tried for a couple weeks to get the Joggins Raft out

Before the advent of self-dumping barges, logs along the Northwest coast were mostly transported by raft. The Davis Raft was especially popular because of its small, maneuverable size.

across the bar and into the Pacific, tug and raft going ashore four or five times in the process before giving up. Finally the more powerful *National City* took over, only to have the raft go completely to pieces in a gale off Cape Mendocino. You'd think such a disastrous experience would be enough to deter anyone from trying again, but the potential for savings and markets was so enticing that another raft was built with ten thousand Douglas fir logs.

Four days after leaving the Columbia River, the logs were scattered all over the Oregon and California coasts, and the unfortunate tug *Monarch* was moored to the bottom by the sixty tons of chains that had held the raft together.

The British Columbia rafts, called Davis Rafts, were a third the size of the ill-fated Joggins Rafts. Their smaller size, and the fact that Queen Charlotte Sound, though rough, was still not as bad as the ocean, allowed successful transport of logs along the north coast of British Columbia.

NAKWAKTO RAPIDS. Perhaps the most isolated and remote section of the whole north coast lies on the eastern shore of Queen Charlotte Sound at Belize Inlet, Nugent Sound, and Seymour Inlet, southeast of Cape Caution. Some of this area is still unexplored, with uncharted rocks. Access to Seymour Inlet, thirty-five miles long, is through Nakwakto Rapids.

The tidal current reaches 16 knots, the highest velocity of any place in North America. On the ebb, the full force of the current hits Turret Rock, which, local lore has it, actually vibrates when the tide is running at strength.

> Vessels are strongly advised to navigate Nakwakto Rapids only at *high water slack*, and due care should be exercised to ensure that the time of this is carefully checked, for at no other time is it possible to navigate these narrows with any degree of safety. If necessary, vessels should anchor in Treadwell Bay, and obtain some practical knowledge of the area by passing through the narrows in a boat at slack water, the time of which should be checked by previous observation from Treadwell Bay.
>
> —*Sailing Directions*

In the early 1930s, Mrs. Muriel Blanchet, the widow traveling with five children in a 25-footer, wanted to go through the rapids and explore the inlet beyond. She met a fisheries officer beforehand who told her he had run the rapids in his power boat twenty minutes after slack.

In all the other rapids on the coast—Seymour, Yuculta, and so forth—you can go twenty minutes after slack and be O.K. Nakwakto is a different story.

The fisheries man said he had barely entered the narrows before the current slammed his stern against a cliff, cleaning off his propeller. For the rest of the tide, the back current along the shore played with his husky 40-foot boat, alternately smashing the bow and then the stern into the rocks, until both were splintered and leaking badly.

Mrs. Blanchet's solution was to anchor around the corner with just enough line out to hold the boat, row a skiff ashore, and climb up to where she could watch the rapids. When slack water came, she ran back through the woods, rowed quickly back to her waiting boat and breathless children, yanked up the anchor, and motored through the narrows before the tide could begin to run the other way.

FITZ HUGH SOUND. Fitz Hugh Sound, on the north side of Queen Charlotte Sound, is where Alaska-bound mariners breathe easier, for this is the entrance to the more sheltered waterways of the Inside Passage. Except for a twelve-mile shot across Milbanke Sound, this protection continues more or less uninterrupted to the Alaskan border, 250 miles away.

For commercial fishermen who have made many passages along this route, the Inside Passage is a commuter highway: they know the turns by heart. They don't even carry charts, except for Alaska. The skippers use something called the *Hansen Handbook,* which contains tables of courses and distances and sketches of the prominent features along the way.

This is great, *as long as you don't stray from the route laid out by the book.* There are no charts to show you where you are if you make the wrong turn.

"It was up around Rivers Inlet, someplace around Fitz Hugh Sound, I dunno, it might have been Fisher Channel that we ended up in. All I really remember is it was the green kid who had been steering; he was from Ohio or somewhere: you know, first summer job in Alaska.

"Hey, it was a straight section of channel, and the rest of the gang was out on the back deck, working on the seine. I figured, how can he screw up, so I showed him where to go and I went and laid down.

"I must have slept two hours, max, and I remember getting up, walking back on deck to have a look around, see how we were coming along, and all of a sudden I thought, *'I've never been here before.'* It was terrifying. I didn't have any idea of where we were, the kid from Ohio was still steering, and we were going full bore. I ran up and took the boat out of gear. He'd missed a turn and gone up one of them side channels for a couple of hours. If I hadn't started not recognizing things, we might have been lost for weeks. That's something a guy sure doesn't want to do too often—wake up on his own boat and not know where the heck he is!"

—A friend

One fall, seeking fuel before crossing Queen Charlotte southbound, we pulled into a cove in lower Rivers Inlet where I heard there was a logging camp. We swung around the point, and there was the town, all built on log rafts, covering perhaps an acre or two. When we got closer, I could see it was abandoned. Some of the houses were sitting at an angle, the water covering part of the floors. There were chicken sheds, overgrown gardens, plants in rotting barrels, clotheslines, bits and pieces of the lives of the families who once lived there.

It was too late to go anywhere else for the night, and dark came on, so we stayed, tied to the logs of that deserted floating town. After supper I stepped out, listening to the creak and groan of the cables that held the raft together, and I looked across at the twisted, tilted, dark and lifeless houses. Earlier, I had walked around the place and found names and dates carved into the buildings' rough siding: "Harold A., 1935," "Biggins, Nov '42," and others more faded and worn, perhaps from the 1920s, I couldn't be sure. I looked out into the black, trying to guess where the raft might have been forty or fifty years before. Perhaps it had been tied to the steep shore of Hardy Inlet to the north or Boswell or Smith inlets in the south.

I imagined the shrill whistle of a steam engine echoing off the walls of a dead-end fjord. I fancied the loggers, staggering down out of the woods, exhausted, to eat in the crudely built bunkhouse. I saw a decrepit steam tug, working its way down the coast, the crew stopping each day to gather fuel wood on shore.

I saw kids playing on the logs with their friends when the little floating camps became tiny towns. When it came time to move, the towns would be towed to new locations.

I thought about such a move, of the children looking curiously as the men brought in the lines that held their homes to the shore. Then the tug taking up a strain, and the logs and the houses themselves starting to creak as the whole works began to move through the water. I thought of them looking at the smudge of smoke the tug left ahead, and watching the bay where they'd played with their friends drop

For some loggers and their families, home was a house on a raft. This floating settlement in Holberg, British Columbia, could be towed from place to place, leaving it free to follow the path of logging's fluctuating fortunes.

farther and farther behind, feeling sadness for leaving, wondering what might lie ahead.

> In the distance, the tugboat that had come from Port Alice to tow away the company buildings and those that would follow the camp to Holberg, tugged and struggled to separate the floats from the shore, much like a dentist pulling teeth.
>
> I went back inside, angry. "What about my memories?" I may not have said exactly that, but it was the essence of what I felt at the time, for until then Spry Camp had been the sum of my experience in the world. I didn't know yet there would be other memories of a childhood raft-life, of snaking up and down Quatsino Sound until each turn was as familiar as a neighbourhood street is to a city child.
>
> —Alan Oman, "The Day They Took Our Town Away," in *Raincoast Chronicles*

Vancouver and Mackenzie. Vancouver and his men finished their 1792 season on the nineteenth of August at Menzies Point in

Burke Channel, which leads northeast from Fitz Hugh Sound. They had come a long way, but they hadn't found the passage they had sought. The vessels headed off to Hawaii for the winter and returned the following June. That summer of 1793 Vancouver missed by a few miles and weeks meeting up with another great explorer of the Northwest, Alexander Mackenzie.

Vancouver, an Englishman who had come halfway around the world by ship, and Mackenzie, a Scotsman who had come across the North American wilderness by foot and canoe, might have had much to say to each other. Each sought a way to connect east and west, Mackenzie by land and Vancouver by sea.

Vancouver's journey, in two large and well supplied ships financed by the Crown, was probably less an ordeal than Mackenzie's. The latter was a fur trader seeking the Northwest Passage in a private journey of trading and exploration.

The slight, but driven, Scotsman had set out from Fort Chipewyan, the westernmost outpost of civilization in Canada, on October 10, 1792. The season for travel in the North was so short and, they suspected, the distance to be traveled so long, that Mackenzie doubted he and his men could make the journey to the coast and back in a single season. So they started in the fall, traveled three weeks, and built a cabin on the Peace River to winter in, planning to get a head start in the spring. Their thermometer froze a few weeks later, a foretaste of the bitter winter they were to endure. When spring came in late April 1793, they set out again, exploring, mapping, but most of all paddling, pulling, and carrying their canoes and supplies up narrower and swifter rivers. They felt their way through the rough wilderness seeking the continental divide, from which Mackenzie hoped the rivers would flow downhill into the Pacific.

After five weeks of arduous travel, they paddled up a narrow, twisting creek on June 12 into a high country lake. Mackenzie noticed with excitement that the lake seemed to be on a ridge, with lower country on all sides. Then, in the early afternoon, they came to the western side of the lake and realized that the streams flowing out of the lake flowed down *to the west*. They had reached the divide!

Exhilarated, and paddling *downstream* for a change, they continued. But nothing came easy. The stream narrowed and grew swifter, canoes capsized, and supplies were lost. A month later, they could see in the distance the faint, shining sea. On July 20, 1793, ten weeks after they had begun and almost totally exhausted and out of supplies, they reached the coast near the present native village of Bella Coola. There they met Indians who told them that white men in great wooden ships had been there shortly before. The leader, the Indians said, was "Macubah," Vancouver. Part of Mackenzie's party set off down the coast, hoping to meet up with the great wooden ships and obtain food and supplies. Unfortunately, Vancouver had headed *up* the coast, and the two explorers never met.

It was a big disappointment. Neither Mackenzie nor his men had anticipated the length or the arduousness of their journey. While Vancouver and his men headed to Hawaii for a winter's rest and rehabilitation, Mackenzie's little band faced a much more bitter prospect. They were exhausted and out of food, but Mackenzie realized the only thing to do was retrace their steps. He painted a sign on a rock, "Alexander Mackenzie, from Canada overland, July 22, 1793," and headed back. His tough and seasoned voyageurs were so worn down he could barely persuade them to get into their canoes for the homeward trek.

On September 4, with the winter hard after them, they arrived back at the little fort they had left four months before. They were hungry, but alive.

When he arrived in Montreal, Mackenzie was already a legend. People crowded around him in the streets to see the man who had made his way to the Pacific and back.

PASSAGES. At Pointer Island lighthouse, not far from where Mackenzie reached salt water, the Inside Passage makes a right-angle turn and enters narrow Lama Pass.

This is a place where the skipper might come forward with a cup of coffee and take over from the crew. This constricted waterway and Seaforth Channel, the next one to the north, have had more than their share of wrecks. The steamer *Mariposa* rammed the shore here in 1915. But as was frequently the case in such strandings, the passengers were picked up by the next passing steamer, and the *Mariposa* was eventually refloated, patched up, and placed back in service.

The *North Sea* wasn't as lucky hitting Porter Reef, a few miles far-ther north, in 1947. The people got off, but the big steel steamer stayed.

This is the place where a 60-foot Japanese sampan appeared out of the mists in July 1913, unloaded six men, and left. The natives at the village of Bella Bella were surprised when the odd craft tied up. The six Japanese, who had paid the skipper fifty bucks apiece to be let off "somewhere near Seattle," were probably even more surprised when they figured out where they were. The sampan crew was lucky to have found British Columbia at all. For charts the boat had a six-by-six-inch map of North America, for instruments an ancient compass consisting of a simple needle balanced on a pivot. The skipper said he was looking for herring, and he headed for Alaska. They left Bella Bella as quickly as they had arrived, disappearing into history.

The Japanese were back looking for herring sixty years later. This time, instead of boats they brought briefcases full of money.

"We were fishing in Skincuttle Inlet that year, and the Japanese buyers went nuts over the fish. The price started out at a thousand bucks a ton, and before we started fishing some of the cash buyers had bid it up to as high as four thousand. Hey, we had never even *seen* some of those buyers before, and we had sets of over a hundred tons. I'm not dumb enough to take a check from some stranger for four or five hundred thousand bucks. So all the fishermen who had the fish in their nets, we got together and said the first guy with the cash got the fish. About three hours after that, the float planes were coming in like kamikazes, trying to land and get the cash over to the buyer before the next plane got there. In each plane was a Japanese buyer with a briefcase full of cash handcuffed to his wrist."

—A friend

West of Seaforth Channel, the steamer channel passes for twelve miles across the head of Milbanke Sound. This part of the journey can be uncomfortable. Milbanke is open to southerly storms, and the tide against the wind makes confused seas. Many smaller boats pursue a more winding route that takes them to sheltered waters north of Milbanke Sound without their having to cross it.

We took Jackson Passage, which is one of those back channels, on November 1, 1974. When we approached the narrow part, I was sure we were headed for a dead end, for the channel seemed to disappear into the trees ahead. Then a way through the trees opened, but it was like a creek through a forest. The branches almost met over our rigging, and at each little turn we frightened hundreds of ducks off the water.

Larger vessels, such as cruise ships, may elect to avoid the narrow channels north of Bella Bella and go up wide Hecate Strait to save a little time.

"We were up in the north end of Hecate Strait, trawling, towing our net along the bottom in a snowstorm, when we saw these fourteen targets on the radar. It was real odd: these targets, the size of ships, just in a straight line, coming up the Sound. At first we thought it was a malfunction in the radar, but then there was a break in the weather and we saw them, a fleet of Russians, big 300-foot trawlers, fishing side by side, towing their huge nets up and down the Sound and throwing nothing back. That was before the 200-mile limit. After those big fellows got done, that was it, there wasn't nothing left for us to catch at all; they'd cleaned the whole bottom for miles and miles."

—A friend

When the wind blows, Hecate Strait can be more like the ocean than a strait. My friend spoke of lying in remote bays in the winter for four and five days at a stretch to get in one day of fishing, and that in an 85-footer.

April 25, 1985, was a good example of why many vessels avoid Hecate Strait altogether.

On that day, a rapidly developing Pacific storm caught weather forecasters and the Canadian halibut fleet by surprise. Five vessels were abandoned or sunk, and the Canadian Coast Guard had to request aid from the U.S. Coast Guard helicopter at Sitka, Alaska. The U.S. chopper arrived to twenty-foot seas, winds gusting to fifty knots, low clouds, and visibility down to less than a half-mile. They had just plucked four cold fishermen from the water and dropped them at Prince Rupert when they learned a second boat was sinking. As they flew to that one, a mayday was heard from a third. Visibility had dropped and the winds and seas had increased, but a Canadian rescue vessel was able to vector the chopper to the two boats and to another one after it. After hoisting crew number four out of the water, the chopper received its fifth distress call of the day. By then, however, they were loaded with survivors—the last three crews were aboard—and unable to make headway against the wind. They did a quick run to Prince Rupert, unloaded, refueled, and headed out again.

By the time they found the last vessel, it was dark, the wind was gusting to sixty knots, and the seas were fifty feet. The chopper managed to hoist all four crewmen before their vessel vanished beneath them.

THE NORTHERN CANYONS. The northern canyons begin at Boat Bluff Light, 439 miles from Seattle, at 52 degrees, 38.6 minutes north latitude. Here vessels pass within the space of a few minutes from Finlayson Channel, two and a half miles wide, into Tolmie Channel, three-eighths of a mile wide, a dramatic transition. Some vessels enter Tolmie Channel through Klemtu Passage, five miles farther south. There the change is even more dramatic, as the channel narrows immediately to less than 600 feet between steep, forested shores.

For the next hundred miles, going north up Tolmie, then northwest into Graham Reach, and into Grenville Channel to Arthur Passage, the waterways are deep and narrow like canyons, whose sides reach frequently to snow-covered tops.

The passage at Boat Bluff Light is so narrow that two large vessels cannot pass in safety. Furthermore, it's a blind corner, and one ship wouldn't even see the other until it was too late.

Nowadays, with all large vessels standing by on the same radio frequency, VHF channel 16, a skipper might call out, "Alaska ferry *Taku* entering Sara Passage northbound. Southbound traffic please advise." In this fashion hazardous encounters are avoided.

Before radios were in common use, large vessels used Hiekish Narrows northbound and Boat Bluff southbound. This protocol kept them from meeting in the narrow channel at Boat Bluff.

On a rainy August night in 1909, the 335-foot steamer *Ohio* was feeling her way up Finlayson Channel, trying to find Hiekish Narrows. Just after 1:00 A.M., she struck an uncharted rock on the south side of the narrows and began filling. The skipper knew his only chance was to call down for full speed and head for Carter Bay to beach his ship. The shore of Carter Bay appeared out of the rainy black just as the ship set-tled onto the shallow beach; it was a close one.

He was lucky to have Carter Bay so close, for most of the shores here are steep, with no place to beach a ship and save its passengers and crew. Vancouver reported finding it more than 600 feet deep a ship's length from shore; he resorted to tying his ship between trees for the night.

And imagine the consternation on the brand-new, 108-foot, steel crabber, *Norseman*, in June of 1978. The helmsman nodded off, and the boat rammed the beach. The crew got off, but the boat, on her maiden voyage, slid off into 400 feet of water and was gone.

The vessel was salvaged by a young diver named Doug Anderson, who said if it hadn't fetched up on a ledge at 400 feet it would have slid another 600 feet to the bottom. Anderson had gotten his leg up in the business a year earlier when he raised a 65-foot vessel from 190 feet of water, using several old railroad tank cars for flotation. There was a fish-eries boom in the Northwest at the time, and vessels of all sorts were in demand. With the proceeds from the sale of the first vessel, Anderson was able to purchase a used tug, with which he salvaged the *Norseman*. After repairing a bulkhead in the bow, Anderson towed the vessel to Seattle, where he quickly sold it for $800,000, almost as much as it had cost new.

On the east side of the channel, eight miles north of Hiekish Narrows in Graham Reach, all that remains of Swanson Bay is the old chimney. In 1916, when the American logger and prospector, W. H. Jackson, stopped there in his rowboat, the 125-foot stack marked a busy town, a center for hand loggers working in much of northern British Columbia. The mills were so eager for timber they would stake a total stranger with a complete outfit for hand logging, including tools, gro-ceries, a boat, even the nails with which to build a cabin.

Today you might go up and down the coast for years before seeing a person in a rowboat, but in the earlier part of the century, Jackson and many others depended on small boats and long oars to get from their

In the 1870s, hand loggers began streaming into northern British Columbia, lured by huge stands of cedar and spruce. Men like these workers near Theodosia Arm favored the area's steep slopes and numerous waterways, which made it easier to dispose of felled trees.

remote homesteads, mining claims, or logging tracts to wherever they got their supplies.

Jackson learned the hand logging trade along this steep coast before working his way north and plying his trade in Southeast Alaska. On occasion he'd drop a tree off a high cliff, and the tree would hit with such force it would drive under water for perhaps a minute before suddenly leaping almost vertically out of the water as it surfaced.

When Jackson rowed into Swanson Bay, he found Swedes, Finns, Australians, French Canadians, Americans, and many other nationalities—in from the woods for a toot or looking for a partner to start a new career in the North.

It's easy to see why this area was so popular with hand loggers. For them, the steeper the terrain, the better. For loggers who worked largely without winches or means other than small screw jacks and gravity to move the trees to the water, this vertical country was ideal.

The trees here, as along much of the British Columbia coast, were giants. Many of the great cedars and spruces were eight feet or more in diameter and the loggers frequently had to start their cut eight feet or more off the ground, wielding their axes and hand saws from springboards, or planks driven into slots cut into the wood. Only by working in this fashion could they make their cut above the base of the tree, where the trunk swells to join the roots.

If a hand logger was lucky, he'd drop his tree so its immense weight and momentum would carry it all the way down the steep slope into the water. More often the tree would be stopped in its headlong rush through the forest as its branches became entangled with other trees.

Then the logger was faced with a very ticklish situation, for he had to work among the branches, cutting away the ones that were holding it back. At any moment, the tree could start sliding again, so the axman had to have an escape route planned, or risk being crushed or swept into the water far below.

On a fair summer day, when the light lingers in the northern sky until almost midnight, these inland waterways of northern British Columbia make a grand and exhilarating passage. Waterfalls tumble down into the salt water on either side of the channel, and thickly forested inlets wind back into the hills. The air smells of the sea and the land.

Coming from the north down Grenville Channel after a difficult crossing of Dixon Entrance, or up from the south and Queen Charlotte Sound through Princess Royal Channel, the mariner can count on an easy journey through these dramatic canyons. In gloomy, wet weather, though, when the bottoms of the clouds press down upon the water, when the rain and the wind darken the winding reaches, the mood on the land and the water can be oppressive.

One's craft feels smaller, one's mood quieter, as if the size and steepness of the mountains, canyons winding on forever, diminish a person. Such a day did so to us in 1982.

Cougar Bay, B.C., October 1982. Anchored in this remote cove at 10:00 P.M., after running some hundred miles from Prince Rupert. The day in shades of gray, with dreary rain, mist and fog layered on the hills and the water. Passed a single troller near Oona River early; nothing the whole rest of the day.

Had planned to keep running through the night, but a thin fog came with the early dark, and to proceed seemed foolish. So found this tiny cove on the east side of Cougar Bay in total darkness by radar, and anchored close to the shore. When the engine was shut down, the rush of a stream sounded very close, and I peered anxiously out into the black. Tonight at supper there was little talk amongst the crew; it was as if the immensity, the loneliness, of the land outside and around had humbled us all.   —Log

Today the Pelton wheel that powered the huge cannery complex at Butedale, British Columbia, is stopped, and the buildings it lit, dark. With the cannery dark, a mariner might well pass this spot without noticing it. But an observant traveler with binoculars will wonder what the buildings are on the south side of the channel, just where Graham Reach swings from north to northwest and becomes Fraser Reach.

For generations this remarkable place was one of the most unexpected sights along the entire Inside Passage, especially in the dark. After passing for hours along shores where the trees started at the water's edge and grew up into the snows, where there was no sign of habitation except for the very occasional navigation lights, to come around the corner and see Butedale all lit up, a whole little town in the middle of the vast wilderness, was a shock.

As late as the 1970s and 1980s, travelers who stopped were even more surprised. The place was deserted except for a storekeeper-caretaker and his family. The lights were left on in the buildings to put a load on the generator, which was driven by water power.

A wooden penstock, or pipe, four feet in diameter, ran up the steep hill behind the cannery. The pipe was tongue-and-groove cedar, banded with iron hoops. At the top, the hoops were several feet apart. Two hundred feet below, where the penstock entered the powerhouse, the hoops were a few inches apart, testimony to the immense pressure of the water within. In several places near the bottom, leaks had been patched with inner tubes held in place with old gill-net web, and here and there water spurted twenty-five feet in the air.

For the coastal mariner, Butedale was a natural stopping place, a long day's run from Prince Rupert in the north or Bella Bella in the south.

One June evening we climbed the stairs that lead to the lake behind the cannery. Beside us the water rushed through the penstock. At the top, we turned left and walked along the lake for a bit. Rotten and half sunk a few hundred yards from the head of the great pipe were houseboats, once homes to the logging crews that worked the lake.

When you stand at the little dam at the top, you can't see the cannery. The pipe falls away out of sight over the brow of the hill, and all you can see is the bay and the narrow channel between the hills that is the Inside Passage. Then you walk a little farther, and suddenly, there at your feet is the cannery, like a fairy-tale city.

One October night we stopped to take advantage of the watchman's offer of a shower. The showers were on the ground floor of the big bunkhouse. Afterward, I went up a floor and walked down a hallway between tidy rooms, each with a dresser, a table, a bed, and a window that gave out on the forest or the bay. Faded pictures of families and girlfriends were pinned to the walls, and the floors and stairs were worn from generations of fishermen and cannery workers. Outside, the fog and the mists swirled around the cannery; it was sad to see it all slowly deteriorating.

Before refrigerated fish-packing vessels made it feasible to transport fish over long distances to canneries in the major towns, such as Prince Rupert, places like Butedale were scattered in inlets up and down the coast. In Rivers Inlet, for instance, a hundred miles or so farther south, there were ten canneries. Thousands of people came from Vancouver and elsewhere to the canneries in northern British Columbia, and the coves were bright with lights, noisy with voices, and throbbing with the sounds of machinery for the summer months.

Each year when we stopped at Butedale, the buildings were more in need of major work, the docks more rotten. In the late 1970s a California group bought it. It was to be a resort, we heard; next it was a hatchery for lobsters. Yet I sensed only the stouthearted Pelton wheel water turbine kept things going, that once the iron hoops that held the penstock together rusted through, or the turbine failed, the lights would go out. The rains and the forest would quickly take over, and Butedale would be like Swanson Bay or a hundred other once-bustling communities along the north coast: just ruins in the forest.

"Yeah, ya jes take that next right, north of Butedale, head up there, take the second bay on your right, and go all the way in. You'll see kind of a log float coming down from the woods; that's the hot springs."

On such skinny advice, Mary Lou, our crewman, and I set out to find the Bishop Bay hot springs. It was late October, and we were heading south after a four-month season. On board was a basic set of charts for the Inside Passage, showing the Seattle-Alaska route, but not much for the channels that branched off in all directions. A half-hour after leaving the beaten path at Kingcome Point, we ran off my chart. The channel stretched ahead, wide and apparently deep, but without charts for it and in a leased boat, I was nervous.

The "second bay on the right" was a gash between the hills, winding back into the forested interior, and as the channel bent around to the south, I wondered if it was the right place, and I began to feel an itch to be back in charted waters. Then at the very head of the bay we saw a ramp down from the steep shore and a float, all made out of rough logs. We eased in and tied up.

We walked a trail and found the hot springs feeding into a cement pool in a cinder block building perched on a rock overlooking the cove.

You may imagine how it felt to sit in that steaming water, while looking out the glassless window openings at our vessel lying so gracefully in the cove below. As we sat in hot water up to our necks, the cares of a long season ebbing away, we heard an odd sound and looked out. For a long time I saw nothing. Then I made out the graceful tails of a pair of humpback whales, lifted for a moment above the still waters of the cove before the animals sounded.

It's too bad Vancouver's Lieutenant Whidbey and his boat crew didn't come a little farther that July evening in 1793 when they were exploring near here. Instead, they stopped for the night at Goat Harbor, the next bay to the south. They found a hot spring there too, but it issued out of the rocks below the high-tide mark and was too hot for comfort. If they had made Bishop Bay before resting for the night, they might have dammed the hot water and made a pool to bathe in. Probably they could have used it.

GRENVILLE CHANNEL. Grenville Channel, 500 miles north of Seattle, is for most travelers the most dramatic part of the passage to

Alaska. Not only does the water narrow to less than a quarter of a mile between very steeply forested walls, but a slight bend makes the channel seem to disappear into the hills ahead and behind. Even the largest vessels can seem insignificant against this dramatic background.

> "We were southbound, Grenville Channel, I think it was, runnin' down to Seattle with a load of halibut. It was blowing like stink outside, so we come on inside. Harald, he was steering that time, he must have fallen asleep, but a tree branch slapped one of the pilothouse windows in, woke him up, he turned the boat and we never even scraped the bottom."
>
> —A friend

And it was here, on a June night in 1981, that a Soviet cruise ship almost crowded us into the shore in the narrowest part of the channel. It was near midnight, cloudy, and very dark when the southbound ship approached, and I called on channel 16: "Hello the cruise ship southbound in Grenville Channel." After several calls there was no answer, and I began to get alarmed, for if anything, the ship seemed to be favoring my side of the channel, beginning to loom over me as she approached. I slowed down to an idle and approached the shore until my rigging was almost in the trees. I couldn't make out the name of the ship, but high in the air above her top deck, a spotlight brilliantly illuminated a huge, red hammer and sickle. I looked up, straining to see into the pilothouse, but couldn't see anyone.

The hum of her engines filled the air and then she passed so close she seemed to graze us. I looked up and for an instant peered right into the plate glass windows of a ballroom, caught a glimpse of couples in long dresses and tuxedos, dancing, peering curiously out into the black. It was eerie—the ship coming through the night, no one answering my radio calls, the red ensign lit up against the black, and then the ballroom full of dancing elite. The ship swept past and I put my boat in gear and pulled away from the shore before its wake arrived.

Old piling on the beach and a few tumble-down buildings in the forest mark the cannery at Lowe Inlet, halfway up Grenville on the east side. This is where the burning steamer *Ravalli* raced with twenty-five YMCA boys and eighty Alaska-bound cannery workers in 1918. It

The massive vessel **Sister Star** *loads logs from a raft near Prince Rupert,*
British Columbia, in 1982.

wasn't a planned stop; the coal bunkers were on fire. The Lowe Inlet
cannery workers were expecting another boat that day and were surprised to see the strange vessel heading full speed into the narrow
entrance, smoke pouring from her holds.

The passengers and crew escaped, but the wood-hulled freighter
burned to the waterline.

PA-AAT RIVER.   Near the top of Grenville Channel, on the west side,
is a white house on a bluff above a small river. It is the first building
visible since Butedale, seventy miles behind.

This is the Pa-aat River. The land changes here, opens up. The
canyonlike feeling so noticeable a few miles to the south is gone. A little
farther ahead is the mouth of the Skeena River, along which runs the
Canadian National Railway. This is the first time the mainland railroad
hits the salt water after leaving the city of Vancouver, 450 miles to the
south.

In the distance one can see the smoke from the mills at Prince Rupert, the commercial center for northern British Columbia. One windy fall, we lay in the harbor waiting for good traveling weather. A few hundred yards from where we lay was a long string of boxcars marked "Canadienne Dept de Ble." It was wheat, thousands of tons of it, from the vast Canadian prairie country over the mountains to the east, waiting for steamers to carry it to Asian ports.

At the head of the dock was a fish-processing facility, in whose storage yard were pallets of small wooden boxes of salmon eggs packed in salt. The colorful printing on the boxes was in Japanese, as the product, and indeed much of the salmon harvested in British Columbia, was for export to Japan.

Out in the harbor was another interesting sight: a Japanese log ship at anchor, her booms swung out to port and starboard. In the water on either side of her were big log booms, and little yard tugs were nudging them against the great ship's wall-like hull.

A dozen or so men scrambled over the logs, fastening the lowered cables to bundled logs, which were hoisted dripping, fresh from the forest, up aboard the ship. In Alaska, not far to the north, such log exports were allowed only if the logs were first sided, or squared up in a sawmill, providing employment at least for the mill crew before the logs left the country.

HECATE STRAIT. The outside passage up this part of the coast is Hecate Strait, forty miles to the west. For the most part, the strait is deep, but at its northern end it shallows to 60 feet in many places.

This is where our new steel crab boat, which had looked so invincible tied to the dock in Seattle, almost came to grief.

It was early March, 1971. As we traveled up Hecate Strait, a southerly gale was building, but it was behind us, and we traveled easily.

I was in the pilothouse; the skipper's brother was on watch. Snow came with the storm, and visibility was down to a few hundred yards. He pored over the chart as he spoke of years in the Canadian trawl fishery, winter fishing in these waters. His voice was gravelly, his hands swollen and scarred. He spoke of two-cent-a-pound fish, of weeks on end with howling winds, of getting out to make a three-hour tow with the net and getting blown back in for two or three days.

Now and then his voice faded away, and his eyes fastened on the windows as an especially large sea lifted the stern and we slid down its flank, engine racing. Breaking crests rode by higher than our windows. Then we were headed uphill again, the engine noise a deeper pitch with the strain. The tops were blown off the seas, white spray and spume lost downwind. On the tops of the seas we were exposed to the full force of the storm. Visibility dropped to nothing, the snow hissed against the windows, the wind screeched through the pipe rigging. A few moments later, we dropped into the trough, and the wind died away to nothing, the snow eddying gently.

In the middle of my afternoon watch, alone in the pilothouse, I began to have a queer feeling of unease that was hard to shake. I scanned the instruments, checked our position twice, but everything was normal. Twice I walked out onto the boat deck and looked astern; row after row of double-stacked crab pots covered the working deck and the wild, smoking seas beyond.

At 3:30 I saw a strange target on the radar where none should have been. It was a wide, blotchy, poorly defined bar that seemed to cover the northern end of the strait, a few miles away. At first I thought it was sea clutter from the storm, but there was something about it that wasn't right. I ran up and down the ranges, hoping it was some electronic trick, but it stayed in the same spot, getting bigger as we approached.

There in that cozy pilothouse, with faint music playing on one of the radios, I began to feel something akin to fear. Outside, there were only gray seas marching past and a snow squall moving in from the east. I pulled the throttle back to half, and the skipper was instantly out of his cabin and up peering into the radar.

He studied it for a moment, fiddled with the controls, glanced at the glowing numbers on the loran, and stalked over to the chart table. Pulling the throttle back to idle, he pushed the intercom button:

"Roger, flood the crab tanks, quick as you can; and let me know the minute they're full."

For greater fuel economy and speed we were running with the crab tanks—almost half the boat—empty. With the load of pots we carried, the onset of heavy weather required that the tanks be flooded for stability.

By then we were less than a mile from the strange target, idling slowly, dead downwind. The cook came up from below, and we peered into the swirling snow ahead.

For a long time there was nothing, just gray seas with white boiling tops. Then, on the top of a big one, there was a break in the squall just long enough to see a solid line of breakers ahead and nothing but white and broken water beyond.

"Shit—hang on!" The skipper swore and pushed the throttle ahead and the steering lever over to starboard in one motion.

Our little ship was built for the worst the North Pacific could dish out. Yet the next sea picked us up like we were driftwood and slammed us down sideways into the trough as we struggled to turn around. I was thrown against the bulkhead, saw green water halfway up the windows, and heard alarm bells go off before we got headed upwind away from the breakers.

The engineer came up a few moments later, looking white around the eyeballs. The alarm had come from the crab tank pumps at the bottom of the boat sucking air. Their intakes were down by the keel.

"Breaking," the skipper said. "For the love of Christ, it's *breaking*, in 80 feet of water. Thirty years up and down the coast, and I've never seen the like of it."

For the next hour we searched among the great seas for the little gully of deep water that should have been there. If it was there, we couldn't find it. The entire northern end of the strait was a seething mass of breakers, as the southerly gale opposed the tide flooding from the north.

The short day ended, and the wind blew harder. And so, in the storm and in the black we had to try to find a way through the islands to the sheltered Inside Passage that lay to the east. We had no chart with sufficient detail of the islands to allow us to navigate with confidence. Instead we relied on the skipper's brother's clouded memory of a trip through those waters a decade before. With such thin information, it was tough to find a passage on such a night. By then it was snowing so hard that our radar could barely penetrate it. (Clutter from the snow makes it difficult to decipher the picture on the screen.)

Several times we approached what we thought was the correct channel, only to have the Fathometer suddenly shallow alarmingly and our glaring work lights reveal seas boiling on hidden rocks. We would back out until the water deepened, turn around, and try another place.

It got very quiet in the pilothouse. There was little talk. You could hear the whine of the wind, the whir of the radar. I hadn't expected to feel fear on such a new and well-equipped vessel. Yet on that black and wild night, as we tried anxiously to find a way out of the building storm, fear was in the pilothouse with us. No one spoke about it, but it was there.

Then the water was deeper and we proceeded. The snow broke for a moment and we got a glimpse of the land on either side of the narrow channel: rocky shores, trees plastered with snow and frozen spray.

The heave of the sea became a little less violent, the howl of the wind a little less shrill through our radar and antennas. After a few more anxious moments, we passed to the inside waters beyond.

The storm passed in the night and gave way to clear, bitter-cold northerly weather. In the thin yellow light of the morning, we saw the mountains of Alaska gleaming in their fresh blanket of snow.

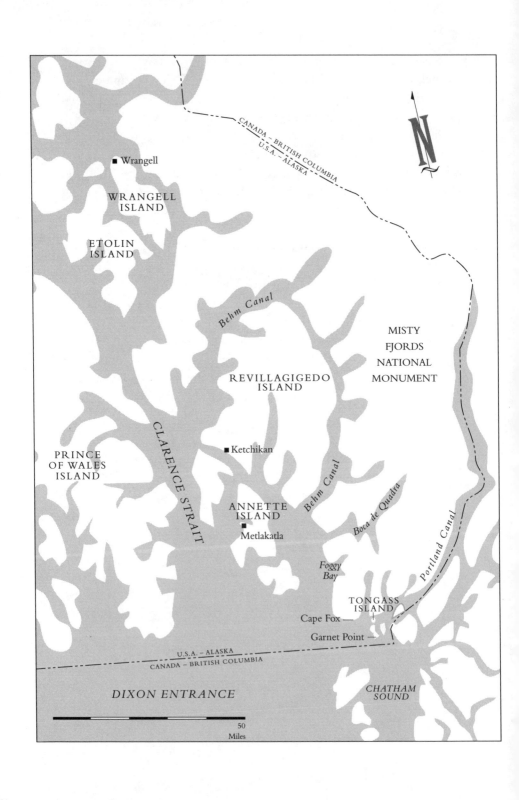

Wrangell

WRANGELL
ISLAND

ETOLIN
ISLAND

CANADA – BRITISH COLUMBIA
U.S.A. – ALASKA

N

Behm Canal

MISTY
FJORDS
NATIONAL
MONUMENT

REVILLAGIGEDO
ISLAND

CLARENCE STRAIT

Ketchikan

PRINCE
OF WALES
ISLAND

Behm Canal

Boca de Quadra

ANNETTE
ISLAND
Metlakatla

Foggy
Bay

Portland Canal

TONGASS
ISLAND
Cape Fox ——
Garnet Point ——

U.S.A. – ALASKA
CANADA – BRITISH COLUMBIA

DIXON ENTRANCE

CHATHAM
SOUND

50
Miles

CHAPTER FOUR

The Windy Border Country

~~~

DIXON ENTRANCE AND
LOWER SOUTHEAST ALASKA

"I WAS ON WATCH, the autopilot was steering, it was the middle of the night. The boat seemed to be starting to list, so I slowed down and went out back to check it out. The skiff and the net were O.K., but then I looked down into the fish hold and saw that the fish were shifting. The guys hadn't put in all the bin boards, and the load had shifted. You could see more fish shifting as you looked at it; it was one of those deals you had to fix right away, or the boat might roll over. There wasn't time to wake the skipper or get the crew up or anything. I jumped down and started throwing fish to the high side. Just after I did, some of the bin boards came out, and the fish started to slide and the list got worse. I was sure someone'd wake up and come down to help me, but no one ever did. I lost track of time.

I must have thrown half of our load [of 40,000 pounds] over to the other side of the boat. Finally, I'd moved enough so that I knew we'd be O.K. I climbed out and looked around; the sun was just starting to come up. I musta' been down there three hours, and we were just idling up on the tenders [the fish buyers]. The skipper got up then, looked around and asked how come we had a list. When I told him, he just looked at me like I was nuts, called out the rest of the guys, and we pulled into the tender to unload. We damn near rolled over, and I don't think anyone even knew it."

—A friend

There are no flags at the border between Alaska and Canada on the Inside Passage. There is no customs station, no duty-free shopping. Along the shores that a traveler might see from the international boundary, except for the iron tower that holds the light at Lord Rock, or perhaps smoke from the native village at Port Simpson, there is no sign of human existence. To the east, the border winds through the rough, steep-sided fjord country; to the west, it crosses the wind-swept and tide-swept waters of Dixon Entrance. Not even a buoy separates Canada from the United States; on the chart it's a dotted line: "approximate boundary."

It's a windy place; one hurries across. There's no reason to linger.

This was the part of the state I came to at nineteen, working as "engineer" on a fish-buying boat. It was June of 1965, and for me it was *ALASKA*—bigger than life, the stuff of books and movies.

ADVENTURES OF THE YOUNG MAN. We tied up to the float next to the Tongass Bar in Ketchikan. The sawmill was down the street. A wall of loggers in spiked boots and red suspenders sat at the bar. Above the bar and around the room were photographs of the fishing fleet: grim-faced men standing by halibut vessels sheathed in ice; graceful salmon boats high and dry on a reef beneath a dark and somber forest. A swarthy group of what I assumed were natives spoke together in a language I could not understand. I nursed my beer until a dispute broke out between a logger who took up two bar stools and a lanky fellow with a white fisherman's cap. With a scraping of chairs, each man's friends stood up. I slipped outside. A moment later I heard raised voices and the tinkle of breaking glass.

At the next bar, a bored-looking woman on a little stage was taking her clothes off. The room was smoky, noisy, and full; the men seemed to pay her little attention. While she languidly stripped, she tripped and fell, bumped her leg, and cried out in pain. No one moved to help her, and after a while she got up and resumed her act.

The next day we traveled to the cannery we were to work for, which was at the Tlingit native village of Metlakatla, on Annette Island, thirteen miles away. I had grown up in East Coast suburbs; nothing had prepared me for such a town. The cannery stood on piling over the bay. The forest and the snow-capped mountains loomed up behind. Bald eagles nested in the tree; seals played by the docks.

My job took me into the cramped engine rooms of the Tlingit seiners. I worked on the big Chrysler Royal straight-eights with the smell of gas so strong in the confined space it stung my nostrils. A dozen feet away in the fo'c's'le, the stocky natives smoked Lucky Strikes and Camels and spoke of ice and rock bays where spirits lurked. I went back aboard our packer with its big well-lit galley and roomy crew quarters suddenly aware that there was a dimension to the land and people around us I had never conceived of before.

The crew on our 90-foot home for the season was the stuff of Alaska fishing lore and legend: the grumpy cook, the insurance man's son as deckhand, and Mickey, the old Alaska salt as mate.

For some reason Mickey liked me, took me under his wing, helped me with the skills I needed to know. The most important was *telling fish apart*. To the casual observer, the twenty-cent-a-pound dog salmon looked almost identical to the sixty-cent-a-pound sockeye or red salmon, especially early in the season. The crews of the boats that sold fish to us, unloading fish rapidly in dimly lit fish holds, were quick to take advantage of this if they could.

"Yah gots ta watch dese boys," Mickey cautioned me, as he squatted by the hatch of a native salmon seiner, a board with three or four mechanical counters on it before him. Below us, three crew members loaded fish as fast as they could into a net bag. For each fish, Mickey's fingers would hit the appropriate counter.

The author first encountered Mickey on a fish-buying boat in 1965, and learned an important skill from him: telling fish apart.

"Yeah, but Mickey, how can you tell the difference?" I whispered in his ear, sure that I would never be as good as he.

When the boat had gone, he laid out four or five fish on the hatch cover and showed me the subtle differences: the shading of the skin, the pattern of the scales, the thickness of the tails.

THE CASH BUYER. Another important skill Mickey taught me was *watching out for cash buyers.*

Our cannery, like many others, had a financial interest in many of the boats that fished for us, sometimes owning them outright. Typically the fisherman delivered his fish to the cannery tender (us) and received his money at the end of the season, less whatever he owed the cannery. However, other fish-buying vessels, not associated with our cannery, and buying fish wherever they could get them, also frequented the grounds, paying cash, giving free beer to all hands, and asking no questions. If one of our fishermen had a particularly good catch and happened to be near a cash buyer, and we weren't around, it would be to his advantage to sell part of it for cash and the rest to us. Our tactic was to anchor in the same cove as the cash buyer or be close enough to the boats that they couldn't sell to another buyer without our seeing them.

"The main trouble with cash buying is you end up carrying so much cash around. It's not so bad in a small boat, when you know all the gang pretty well. But in '68, we were cash-buying with a floater [a processing vessel] with thirty guys on board, and we didn't have a safe. Well, usually we had at least sixty or eighty thousand bucks in the cash box. So each night before I hit the sack, I'd hide the cash box in a different spot. You can imagine how many places there are to hide a cash box in a 120-foot floater. Then one morning I forgot where I'd put it. *I couldn't find the cash box!* I was wild! I spent the whole day hunting for that sucker before I found it. I got a safe after that!"

—A friend

Most of all, Mickey shared four or five decades of experience with me. On my wheel watches, he'd be up in the big pilothouse, watching the chart, his husky voice telling tales of towns abandoned and vessels and crews lost before I was born.

We picked our way into the tiny entrance to Myers Chuck in Clarence Strait, and Mickey's voice was soft; I had to strain to hear the words. It was 1920 or 1922, and he was a deck hand on the mail boat run out of Ketchikan, in and out of a dozen little settlements that are now ruins on the beach.

"The skipper, see, he'd have the pilothouse window open, and the snow'd be swirling right in around us. He'd reach up, pull on the whistle cord, just once, quick-like, and then stick his ear right out into the snowy black and listen for the echo. Then he'd put the throttle to her for a minute or two, then cut back, and do his little whistle trick again. Do that four or five times, and then suddenly he'd turn to us standing there. 'O.K., boys, get the lines out.' We'd look out and there would be nothing but snow. Then he'd reverse, and we'd bump right into the dock before you could ever see it."

Or the deck hand and I, ashore in the skiff in a lonely bay, might discover the ruins of buildings in the woods. Mickey would have the story, "Oh, yeah, that's the old Northwestern Whaling Company's station. They had three steam whalers stationed here in '33. Torvald Jensen was the highline harpooner." He would go on for ten or fifteen minutes about the exploits of men and whales three decades before.

My job was to keep the two main engines, two auxiliary engines, and all their associated systems operating properly. I had really wanted the job badly, so I had substantially exaggerated when the skipper asked about my experience. "Oh, sure," I'd said suavely, "I've worked on plenty of reefer systems." In reality, I'd only been on one other refrigerated boat, and that as second engineer. Furthermore, that vessel had an ammonia system, very different from the Freon system on the salmon tender.

I had a bad habit for a person working around refrigeration equipment, that of unconsciously sticking out my tongue, just the smallest bit, when I was concentrating or anxious. One day, while I was making an adjustment on the system, I was getting a bit worried as it didn't seem to be working as it should. Without thinking, I had my tongue out, and the tip of it touched one of the refrigerant lines and froze to it instantly. First I tried to thaw it off with my other hand, then tried to push it off with a screwdriver, which didn't work either. Meanwhile the system pressure was rising, and I had to declutch the compressor from the engine, but couldn't reach the handle. Frantic, I ripped my tongue off the line, pulled the clutch lever, shut down the auxiliary engine, and looked at the place where my tongue had been prisoner. There were three tiny taste buds, frozen on.

After I had cleaned up and gone to the galley, the cook greeted me, "Hey, look at these, best-looking steaks I've seen all season." I couldn't taste a thing.

On the docks in Seattle, when I'd been looking for a job, young men spoke of the good times they'd had in the towns and bars up north; the bars were where many of the crews spent their time when they weren't fishing. No one spoke of the immensity of the land, of the islands without number.

Our beat was the remote coves and lonely bays where our boats sought the salmon, and the long channels between them and the cannery.

A catch of king salmon from Sea Otter Sound.

The cook didn't steer. The skipper didn't trust the insurance man's kid. Mickey's eyes weren't good in the dark. So on our long runs, I steered much of the night.

In the fall we'd buy fish in Icy Strait, twenty hours from our cannery. We'd finish up after dark. I'd run the anchor winch and then go below to check things in the engine room before cleaning up. I'd get a mug of coffee at the galley on the boat deck, behind the pilothouse and the skipper's quarters. Then I'd step into the pilothouse and let my eyes adjust to the dark, which was broken only by the faint illumination of the compass, radio, and radar. The skipper would show me where we were on the chart, tell me where we were headed and when to wake him, and retire.

We'd have made the turn into Chatham Strait by then. Ahead would be only black. Behind the same. On the radio would be the faint, faraway sound of a Seattle rock station fading in and out. If it was cloudy, only with difficulty could you tell the night sky from the land, the sea from the shore. Only the pale trace of the land on the radar screen was there to guide us. When it was clear, the northern lights shimmering brightly would illuminate the canyon we steamed through.

Our skipper knew all the tricks of the fish-buying business. On our first trip out of town to the "grounds," the bays where our boats were fishing twelve hours away, we anchored up for the night in a forested cove.

"Here," our skipper said, handing me a box of brand-new injectors, sort of the spark plug in diesel engines, "put these in after supper. Make sure you clean up the old ones real well, and put them back in the same boxes." I did as I was bid, wondering why the old ones had to be cleaned up so well if they were going to be sent back to be rebuilt anyway. In the morning I found out.

We pulled up to one of the first boats we came to. Our skipper hailed the other skipper. "Watch this," he said, giving me a sly wink.

"Here's those new injectors you ordered," he said, passing him the box with the injectors I had taken out the night before. "Good luck out there today."

We supplied our boats with grub the cannery purchased for them, because they spent much of their season away from the few towns in the region. To this end, we had a huge storeroom filled with groceries, soda, cases of paper towels, and so forth. Out of each order that went to the boats, a little would be set off to one side. At the end of the season, those little extras amounted to a couple of pickup truck loads that went straight to the skipper's garage. That's called "Save the best stuff for home."

But he saved the best trick for last. It was called "Skip out and don't pay the gang." When we got to Seattle the skipper gave me a hundred bucks to get the boat unloaded, and he split. I finally figured out he was hoping I would leave town for college before he had to pay me. Only by pleading and cajoling him repeatedly on the phone did I get my money.

How could I know that a decade and a half later I'd be a fish buyer in the same region, and that the lessons I learned that summer would serve me so well? On my first day as skipper of a fish-buying vessel, almost the first customer was an authentic red-faced Norwegian fisherman. He unloaded a thousand pounds or so of what I had assumed were twenty-cent-a-pound dog salmon. But when I'd made out the receipt, he turned to me angrily, "Vot's dis, young fella? Dese be reds, by gum!"

I felt my face flush; at first I thought he was right, that I'd made a mistake, that the word would quickly get around the fleet that I didn't know my fish.

But then I looked more carefully and realized that I wasn't really sure *what* they were. Yet if I bought a load of dogs and paid red prices (almost three times as much), my days as fish buyer might be over as soon as they started.

I remembered the tactic Mickey had taught me, the one you used when you were really stumped. I went into the galley, brought out my sharpest fillet knife, made the tiniest cut along the belly in one of the fish, and looked at the color of the flesh in relief. Instead of the bright red of a sockeye, it was the pale, almost cream color of a dog.

"Well, maybe you should find another buyer if you think these're reds."

A long while passed. "Huh," the fellow finally replied, somewhat more humbly. "Guess they're dogs."

Our leased 70-footer served as a mother ship to a dozen smaller boats gill-netting for salmon out of Lincoln Channel, near the British Columbia border. Our base was a cannery in Petersburg, twenty hours to the north. On Saturday night, after taking on ice, fuel, groceries, mail, and whatever supplies the fishermen needed, we'd leave Petersburg for the run south, arriving the following evening, and anchor in a cove on Sitklan Island. Our boats would come in to deliver fish and pick up supplies as soon as we arrived.

Each day during the "fishing period" (typically Sunday noon until Wednesday noon), we'd travel a route, making several stops for the smaller gill-netters to come alongside to unload. In the late afternoon, we'd return to the cove where we started, and the bulk of our little fleet would come in to deliver their fish in the evening.

In years with a lot of fish, the long run from Petersburg to Garnet Point, on Lincoln Channel, can be a grueling ordeal. Fishing is often extended to five days a week, and the tenders fill after two or three days. Then they have to either transfer their fish to another vessel or make a quick trip to town to unload; there's barely time to get fuel and head out again. Either way, it makes for a long week, with fifty or sixty hours of steaming plus the fish-buying duties. But the years we tended the south end were slow ones, the weather was unusually good, and we took advantage of the abundant free time to beachcomb and explore.

*One century ago, visitors to Tongass Island found haunting totems marking the
entry to a thriving Tlingit village. Now, only rotted poles remain among
towering spruce trees, and a few trading beads lie scattered along the beach.*

On a calm day, we anchored off the wild and isolated Lord Islands
and stood for a long while in a copse of stunted spruce watching a com-
pelling drama. A group of orcas, or killer whales, were charging back
and forth in the constricted passages, trying for a furry supper of seal
pups. At times we thought the killer whales would beach themselves,
so aggressively did they seek the seals.

Exploring the south side of Tongass Island we found rotting totem
poles in the woods behind the cove. And at the little beach a mile north
of Garnet Point we found trading beads: perfect, eight-sided, dark
purple crystals by the coffee-can full. We searched the beach on hands
and knees for beads.

It was from this beach, a native friend told us, that the Tlingit
villagers set out on their trading and hunting journeys up and down the
coast. Their custom before such voyages was to cast a necklace or two
into the water as an offering to the gods for a safe and successful
journey.

After an hour or so of searching, we found the first tiny beads, barely larger than a large grain of sand, red, blue, yellow, and green, with holes drilled through their centers. A little later we found four so-called "Russian" beads together, as if the necklace holding them had but recently rotted away, keeping the beads from being scattered in the winter storms. These were larger, perhaps five-eighths of an inch in diameter by a half-inch deep, octagonal; they were cobalt blue.

At first I thought the natives foolish for casting these treasures to the sea. But a few days later, as we got under way after nightfall deeply loaded with fish, feeling the bow lift into the seas and hearing the wind start to howl in the rigging, I understood their feelings better.

Farther south on another day, we looked for Japanese glass balls along the wild beaches north of Cape Fox. We anchored in the cove behind the light at Tree Point, explored the abandoned group of Victorian buildings that made up the light station before it was automated.

One of the few bad parts to the fish-packer job was that when you had a load of fish to take to the cannery, or gas and food to take to waiting fishermen, you had to go, unless the weather was really terrible.

And so one night we found ourselves trying to feel our way into the harbor at Foggy Bay in thick weather, black of night, and an onshore gale. Our 65-foot boat was deeply laden, struggling, and making slow progress. The prudent mariner would have stayed in the shelter of Ketchikan harbor, thirty miles to the north, but we were carrying food and supplies the fishermen badly needed, so we had to keep on.

The tide was low and the entrance was constricted to about a half-mile wide between reefs. Normally, making that approach in thick weather, you parallel the De Long Islands, a half-mile off. Then when the half-mile range ring on your radar almost touches the shore on the south side, you make your right-angle turn into the bay. Ideally, such an "instrument landing" clears the reefs on either side of the entrance with a few hundred yards to spare. It sounds easy, but in heavy weather on a black night, with a big sea going and rain like someone was outside hitting your boat with a fire hose, the radar screen fills with clutter and deciphering it becomes difficult. As we turned at what I thought was the right place, our new course put us into the trough of the seas, and our forty-year-old wooden boat groaned with the stress of the

120,000 pounds of water and ice we carried.

Mary Lou, six months pregnant with our first child, came out of the tiny stateroom to stand beside me, as did our engineer. We peered ahead to catch a glimpse of the cheering lights of boats at anchor in sheltered waters. I turned off the compass light and the instrument lights to allow our eyes to penetrate the night outside. But there was nothing—no twinkle of lights, no glimpse of stars overhead, no faint line between sea and sky, no shadow of land. Only impenetrable darkness, slashing rain, and angry seas pounding on all sides. The radar screen was an indecipherable mass of targets, and when a sea larger than the rest slammed our craft heavily sideways, I could only hope that I had allowed properly for the effect of the tide and the wind on our course. No one spoke, yet all knew keenly the hazards that awaited us if we were swept off course, and it seemed a very long time before the worst of the seas had died away, and we knew we had cleared the dangers.

When we had made the shelter of the inner harbor, and the anchor was down and the engine off, we could hear, even over the wind and the rain, the sea booming on the outside reefs. The passage that had seemed so wide on a fair day was like threading a needle on that night.

Misty Fjords. This first part of the Alaska coast, to the east of the steamer track, up the mainland shore from the border almost to Ketchikan, is all part of the Misty Fjords National Monument. Most travelers pass without realizing the existence of the intricate waterways and inlets that lie to the east.

But for the adventuresome mariner in a small boat, this whole area—Hidden, Winter, Willard, Fillmore and Nakat inlets—presents an opportunity to travel and explore little-visited waterways in true wilderness. Here are steep-sided inlets with narrow entrances, winding channels with dramatic and ever-changing panoramas at each turn.

Vancouver's men had a particularly frustrating time along this section of coast. Following the mainland shore, they had to make sure they didn't pass up any inlet that might lead to the Northwest Passage.

For example, it is only seventeen miles from the British Columbia mainland at Rushbrook Pass to the U.S. mainland at Cape Fox. But if you follow the shore up and down all the inlets, the distance is more like 300 miles. North of Winter Inlet, the eastern entrance to Pearse and Portland canals is less than 1,000 feet wide. It widens then and becomes a deep fjord, winding between 5,000- and 6,000-foot mountains and extending north for seventy-five miles.

Before 1959, when Alaska became a state, the Territory's south end (as this part of Southeast Alaska is known) was home to very large runs of pink and chum salmon. At that time, most of the fish were taken by floating fish traps. A trap was an arrangement of anchors, logs, chains, and nets set off a point where fish were known to school. A leader of netting would be hung from buoys or piles, leading to the beach from the main part of the trap. The fish, traveling along the shore, would hit the leader and travel along it until they entered the main part of the trap, a maze from which it was difficult to exit.

Each day, a trap-tending vessel would remove the fish and take them to the cannery. One day a week fish were allowed to pass through the trap to allow enough fish to escape to spawn and provide for the next generation.

Naturally, the traps were expensive to build and maintain, and their ownership tended to be concentrated in the hands of a few wealthy cannery operators. Many of the canneries were owned by men from Seattle, which Alaskans called "Outside"; they were non-Alaskans.

The outside ownership of fish traps and the rich fisheries being administered from Washington, D.C., were two of the burning issues that led to Alaska statehood.

Generally, each trap had a watchman aboard, living in a shack, so other fishermen wouldn't steal the fish. The watchmen weren't paid very much, and there were ample opportunities for them to supplement their incomes by allowing pirate fishermen to help themselves, for a fee. This was so prevalent that at one time the trap watchmen openly discussed a set fee for such late-night transactions.

Today, except for those the Tlingits are permitted to own at Metlakatla, the fish traps are gone, but the tradition of the fish pirates lives on. The state hires college biology students to count the fish going up streams and, by their presence, to discourage fishermen from illegally fishing at the mouths of the creeks, where the fish are apt to be schooled up.

"Hey, I was just a biology student, I was just there to count fish and make sure no one was fishing beyond the markers. Well, the third week of July, the humpies [a species of salmon] were getting thick, just milling around in a big school just above the markers. Well, one foggy evening I could see the lights of a boat out there, and by and by I heard a skiff coming ashore. Two guys were in it, big guys. They came right up to me. One of the guys had a fistful of cash and the other had his rifle.

"'We're giving you a choice, college boy,' the bigger of the two guys said. 'You can either take this money and take a hike while we fish, or,' he jerked his head over at his pal carrying the rifle, 'we'll just shoot you and leave you for the bears.'

"Hey . . . it was getting dark . . . I couldn't see their boat's name, both of the dudes looked alike . . . What was I supposed to do, get a bullet in the gut saving a couple thousand humpies. So I took a hike."

—A friend

The stream watchers had to deal with bears as well. A bush pilot landed on a remote beach on Admiralty Island with two such young men and their tents and gear for a summer of counting fish. Of all the islands in Southeast Alaska, Admiralty is the one most full of bears.

The pilot eyed the kids' gear for a bit before saying, "Where's yer gun?"

"What d'ya mean? No one said anything about needing a gun." They looked surprised.

"Didn't they tell you how bad the bears were here?"

The two college men looked a little pale.

"Yeah, they got brownies here; they're bad."

The pilot turned back to the plane and fumbled around until he found a pistol.

"Here," he said, handing it to them, "take this. It's only a .38, it won't stop a brownie, but you can shoot yourselves with it if you get cornered."

KAZUNOKO MADNESS. The first lighthouse one sees after crossing the border from Canada is at Tree Point. The next bay to the north is Foggy Bay. Each spring, this part of the coast is the scene of one of the more bizarre fisheries in the state, which some call Kazunoko Madness. Kazunoko is the Japanese term for the product of this fishery—the salted egg, or roe, sacs of the herring that spawn here. It is only a one- or two-day fishery, and a stranger wandering into the peak of it might think he had blundered onto the set for an Alaskan *Star Wars*.

Each year at the end of March, beginning of April, a strange variety of craft gathers for it. The flagships are the processors: 200- to 300-footers with helicopters whirring on and off their decks. The processors are served by dozens of smaller fish-buying vessels. But it is the fishing craft, called herring skiffs, that seem so bizarre.

In many Alaska fisheries, graceful, nicely painted craft, well-maintained, harvest the product. This fishery isn't one of them. Herring skiffs are ugly, boxy, totally open skiffs designed to pack as much herring as possible, take a lot of knocks, and keep on working. The first skiffs were little more than plywood boxes with outboards on the back, but then aluminum became the material of choice.

> "Yeah, that's all we had in the beginning, one of those plywood skiffs with an old Johnson 18, that was really back in the hand-to-mouth days. Well, we had to upgrade so we built an aluminum skiff just at the time when things were really taking off. Ah, I guess we've grossed almost a half a million bucks with that skiff in the past four years, but it's just a livin'."
>
> —A friend

The stressful part of the business is it's a quota fishery. The state biologists make an estimate of the herring mass each year and pick a certain small percentage of it as the allowable catch, or quota.

Then comes the waiting, for the fish can be properly processed only if they are taken when they are "ripe," or ready to spawn. For the biologists, it's a tough call. If they allow the fishermen to fish too soon, the fish won't be worth much; if they wait too long, the fish might spawn and be worth even less. An immense school of herring, many thousands of tons, can ripen and spawn in a matter of hours.

Such elements make herring fishing a real hurry-up-and-wait

When the price of herring roe skyrocketed in the early 1980s, skiffs might approach a tender bearing 25,000 pounds of fish. Sometimes the lucrative haul was the result of only a few hours' work.

business. In March 1982 we were in Seattle, leisurely loading freight aboard our 70-footer to take up to the Petersburg cannery we worked for, when the word came down: "The fish are getting ready to spawn at Kah Shakes, hurry up and get there, hurry, hurry!" Kah Shakes is a cove north of Foggy Bay.

So we got the last things aboard, threw off the lines, and headed north, stowing things as we went, traveling around the clock seven hundred miles to Petersburg. There the waterfront was in an uproar, as thirty or forty big boats rushed to unload their freight and put aboard the fish pumps and other equipment needed to buy herring with.

So after steaming nonstop sixty-five hours to the cannery, we worked through the night to get the freight off and the fish pump and other equipment on, and then headed off fifteen hours south to Kah Shakes.

When we finally got there and got the anchor down, all I wanted to do was to go ashore for a walk someplace where I didn't have to listen to boat engines. But even to go ashore in the skiff for a walk, I had to carry a walkie-talkie clipped to my belt in case our fleet manager suddenly called with instructions to head off somewhere else.

That night over the radio we got the word that the fish weren't as ready as had originally been thought, that it might be a while before the fishing began. At that, I called up a friend in another big boat, and we both pulled our anchors and snuck away ten miles to a secluded spot called Weasel Cove to fish for crab, shoot hooters, and just get away from the city of light and noise that Kah Shakes had become.

A week later we were still waiting. By then we had moved to the inner part of Kah Shakes Cove, jammed full of vessels of all sorts, also waiting. In the middle of the night, the noise of another boat coming alongside woke me up, and I got out of my bunk to find another big fish-packer there: "Hey, we need to borrow some of your gear, they say Sitka's about to go off." Sitka is another herring fishery, but for seiners, larger vessels than gill-netters. After he left with what he needed, I looked into the outer anchorage where night was being turned to day with the brilliant iodine-quartz lights of forty or fifty big boats coming on all at once, as the vessels got ready for the twenty-two-hour run out to Sitka. So many started up, turned on their radars and turned on their crab lights all at once that everyone was blinded, and even the radars weren't of much help, being full of interference from all the other radars. One vessel hit a reef.

"Ya get a lot of snow around Kah Shakes in March and the beginning of April, not steady, but a lot of squalls—like, you know, snow hard for maybe ten minutes, then the sun'll come right out?—that kind of stuff, all day long. Well, we were waiting there one year in the snow, and those fish were almost ready to pop. Then about 10:30 in the morning, the snow stopped all of a sudden, and my God, you would have thought you were on the deck of an aircraft carrier or something, so many float planes suddenly started up and took off!"

—A friend

Twenty-four hours later, another sort of noise in the night woke me up, a sound like rain on the water. I stumbled out into the pilothouse, wondering what sounded so odd. Then I realized it wasn't rain at all, but the sound of millions of little herring tails beating on the still water in the cove. The fish were moving into the shallows, a good sign.

The fishing is done with shallow gill nets, from which the herring are shaken by hand or by mechanical shakers. Once the fishing starts, it will usually be over in forty-eight hours or less. Under this kind of pressure, it behooves a fisherman to use every advantage he can; many pay spotter pilots to help them see where the hottest action is.

In the mid 1980s, when it seemed the Japanese would pay any price for herring roe, a lot of money was made here during those few days. At the peak of it, when the price approached two thousand dollars a ton, some of the hot shots were putting in twenty-five or thirty tons in a forty-eight-hour opening!

For many herring fishermen, the season begins in San Francisco Bay, where they work out of the Sausalito waterfront for a few weeks in December and January. This isn't too bad a berth. In the boom years there was so much money to be made buying and selling herring roe that buyers set up hospitality suites in the hotels and prowled the docks with briefcases full of cash.

> " 'Frisco . . . jeez, when we started down there, it was gravy, a guy could go out and get thirty, forty tons some years, and they were paying two thousand bucks a ton, plus you'd get to eat in all those fancy restaurants; it was good money back then. Today, you don't get those real big smashes anymore. You go down there, you might get twenty tons, and the price's down to a thousand bucks [a ton], but still, for a couple of weeks in the winter when you're not really doing anything anyway, what the hell?"
>
> —A friend

From San Francisco, the guys will truck their boats to Seattle and load them aboard fish packers for the trip to Kah Shakes. Then it is back aboard the packer again for Prince William Sound, Togiak, and finally Norton Sound, the last stop on the herring circuit.

Norton Sound is the lonely bay north of the Yukon River delta, near the Arctic Circle. The herring regulars and the Yupik-speaking natives bump elbows here for a few short weeks, frequently working on the southern edge of the ice pack, until the quota is caught and herring fishing is over for the year.

For the Japanese, an even more desirable product than herring roe is roe on kelp. The herring eggs, when released into the water, attach themselves to kelp fronds, in an even, smooth coating. These egg-laden fronds used to be harvested by divers. However, the product was worth so much, and the fishery turned into such a frenzy, that the state banned the harvest of roe on kelp in this part of Alaska. Imagine cutting a bunch of kelp that herring have laid their eggs on, salting the kelp carefully into buckets, and then selling the whole mess for twenty bucks a pound!

The demand for the product remains so strong it pays fishermen to harvest the kelp without the roe, fly it in a chartered 737 to Prince William Sound, and suspend it from frames in salt-water coves, trying to catch herring spawn on the kelp there.

BOCA DE QUADRA. Just north and around the corner from Kah Shakes Cove is the dramatically beautiful, many-armed fjord called Boca de Quadra. Winding thirty miles deep into the interior among snow-covered mountains, Boca de Quadra and the next three fjords to the north, Smeaton Bay, Rudyerd Bay, and Walker Cove, make the centerpiece of the Misty Fjords wilderness area.

Busy in the summer with tour boats and fishing boats, the area waits until winter to show its full beauty, when the snow covers the mountains down to the water. Then the Boca is deserted, visited by a handful of boats fishing for shrimp and crab in an area the size of some New England states.

It is also the center of an ongoing controversy between a foreign-owned mining concern and the fishing and environmental community of Southeast Alaska.

In the steep and little-visited country to the north of the Boca, a prospector uncovered what turned out to be a huge body of molybdenum ore, or "moly." Rio Tinto Zinc, an English company, began to develop the claim and make plans to open one of the largest open-pit mines in the world. Naturally such an immense project caused alarm to fishermen. The plan called for material removed from the pit to be crushed for the ore and the flourlike residue, or tailings, to be dumped into the deep waters of the Boca.

Earlier, a similar tailings disposal scheme had been used for a moly mine on the west coast of Vancouver Island, British Columbia. Fishermen there asserted that the dumping of the tailings had created a marine desert out of a once-productive inlet.

Of course, the Ketchikan town fathers believed that the moly mine would bring new prosperity to their town. It would mean a steady economic base without the ups and downs of logging, fishing, and tourism. Environmentalists, on the other hand, tended to believe the promises of future prosperity were vastly exaggerated, if not outright lies.

The jobs have never materialized. Rio Tinto Zinc's subsidiary, U.S. Borax, has stopped work on the project, waiting, they say, for the international moly market to improve. However, much of the preliminary work has been done and a dock and a road have been built. Whether the mine will ever go into production remains to be seen. The dock and the access road are fifty miles from the nearest town, Ketchikan; it would be a very expensive place to put a mine.

Most people who visit the Boca wonder how any land manager could consider putting such a major and obtrusive project into such a dramatically beautiful and pristine area. Or if the project were allowed, how permission could be given to dump an immense volume of possibly toxic tailings into the salt water.

This issue of resource extraction was a bone of contention when the Alaska National Interest Lands Conservation Act was debated in 1979 and 1980. Many fishermen, environmentalists, and others felt that the Boca was an entirely inappropriate place for such a huge mine.

That the project has come as far as it has reflects the power of money and lobbyists and their ability to grandfather-in mining claims in a designated wilderness area. Opponents at first couldn't believe the government would allow mining there. Later, they were surprised at how little power they had to stop it.

"Well if there are no crab or shrimp on the bottom, there are sure a hell of a lot that crawl into my pots on the way up."
—Testimony of a Ketchikan fisherman at a hearing after a biologist asserted there was little of commercial value on the bottom of Boca de Quadra.

A hand troller at work in Sumner Strait.

One evening I listened to a friend on his yachtlike fish boat, lying at anchor behind Gannet Island. Outside was the Boca: silent, immense, shining in the starlight.

"I could have stopped it five years ago," he said after a long while. He knew the Boca's watery secrets; in the winter, he fished its most distant corners for crab and shrimp.

"How?" I asked.

"Wilson Arm," he said, nodding his head off to the north, where a string of nameless peaks rose to snow and ice. "I used to lay up in Wilson Arm, winters, shrimping. It's another fjord, like this one, over the other side of the mountain. I kept seeing a little cruiser in there, an old one, all varnish and windows, not like what you'd expect to see up here at all. So I went alongside him one day, gave him a mess of crabs, visited for a bit, asked what it was that he was up to. He said he was a prospector, and I thought nothing of it. Then later I found out he was the guy that found the moly. I wish I'd known about it. I shoulda' taken care of it then and none of this bullshit would be happening."

I didn't get it. I didn't understand how he could have taken care of it, when millions of dollars and teams of fishery and environmental lobbyists hadn't been able to stop it. I asked him what he meant.

He got up and stood for a moment with his back to me, staring at the haunting scene outside, the aurora starting to play in muted colors over Marten Arm and lonely Hugh Smith Lake, over Fools Point and Tombstone Bay, the vast and seldom visited land to the east.

A gust of wind shook the boat again, and he looked at me for a long moment. Only later did it strike me what he might have been thinking: how much easier all their lives would have been, how much money and years of futile struggle could have been saved, if an accident had happened to the prospector and his boat in that lonely bay on that winter morning.

GOING TO TOWN.   Working in the south end as we did, exploring so many of its nooks and crannies, we got to appreciate it for the stark and unusually beautiful place it was. During the salmon season, things in Petersburg and Ketchikan verge on the chaotic, and each time we savored our return to the quiet and beauty of the south end.

One August after an evening run up Revillagigedo Channel into Ketchikan, we lay for a few minutes at the float by the Tongass Bar to stretch our legs and let off a passenger.

As my wife and I stood at the edge of a dock, a fellow appeared around the corner, walking unsteadily, and headed for the door of the bar. He missed by a good yard, walked smack into the wall instead, and slumped to the ground, unconscious. A moment later an unmuffled pickup truck with oversized "Bigfoot" tires lurched to a brake-squealing stop at the light. Three young men were inside and the tape deck was playing acid rock at full volume. They threw a couple of empty beer bottles out onto the street before the light changed and then lurched ahead, around the corner, weaving until they were out of sight.

A couple appeared, stopped, and sat arm in arm on one of the benches on the dock. "At last," I murmured to Mary Lou, "someone who's not drunk or stoned."

The man lurched for the woman; she resisted. Then they tumbled off the bench into the broken glass that littered the dock.

Twenty minutes later we were northbound again, steering from up on the flying bridge, putting the lights of town behind us as we headed out into dark and beckoning Clarence Strait. The last of the color was fading from the sky to the west; our brief stop in town seemed like a weird dream.

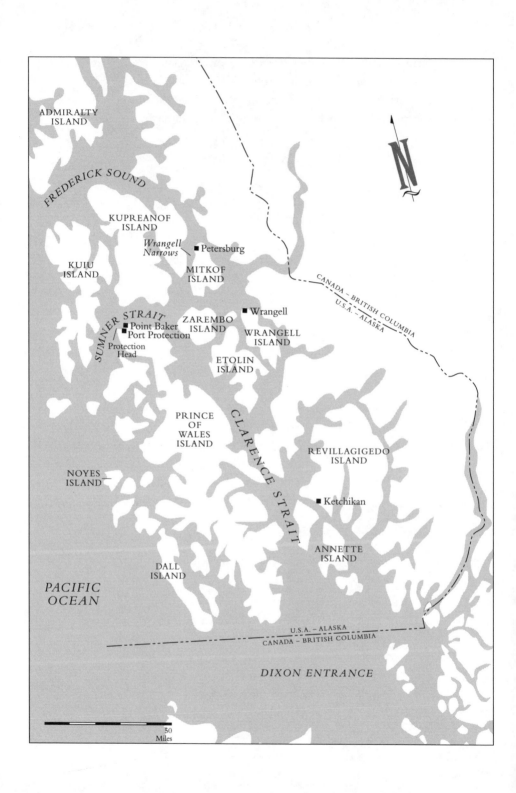

ADMIRALTY
ISLAND

FREDERICK SOUND

KUPREANOF
ISLAND

KUIU
ISLAND

*Wrangell
Narrows* ■ Petersburg

MITKOF
ISLAND

SUMNER STRAIT

■ Point Baker
Port Protection

Protection
Head

ZAREMBO
ISLAND

■ Wrangell

WRANGELL
ISLAND

ETOLIN
ISLAND

CANADA – BRITISH COLUMBIA
U.S.A. – ALASKA

PRINCE
OF
WALES
ISLAND

CLARENCE STRAIT

REVILLAGIGEDO
ISLAND

NOYES
ISLAND

■ Ketchikan

ANNETTE
ISLAND

DALL
ISLAND

PACIFIC
OCEAN

U.S.A. – ALASKA
CANADA – BRITISH COLUMBIA

DIXON ENTRANCE

50
Miles

N

CHAPTER FIVE

Islands Without Number

KETCHIKAN TO PETERSBURG

"**How could I forget** that night Stormy was born? We were beach logging that winter, that whole stretch from Ratz Harbor down to Thorne Bay, and living in a tent on the shore. Each day we'd be out there from first light until dusk, trying to get those big ones off the beach. Sometimes we'd work a whole day just getting the one log off. You'd have to cut smaller logs to skid them with, and then use the big screw jacks, just a couple of inches at a time until finally you got them down where the tide could reach them. George, he had a big saw, with a forty-eight-inch bar on it, and he could barely get through some of those logs, going both ways, that's how big they were. But what wood—beautiful, straight-grained stuff, the kind they call piano spruce. If [the logging company] had known the kind of wood along there, they would never have sold us the rights so cheap. Or maybe they just figured it was so exposed along there that no one could ever get them logs off.

"Four months we worked to get the raft together. It was going to be a good paycheck, and we were talking about buying some land or a new boat.

"I went into labor the day before the tug came to tow the raft over to the sawmill. George called for a plane with the CB we had in the tent. I don't think the pilot would have even tried to get in, the wind was blowing so bad by then, if he didn't know that my baby was coming. He finally set her down on about the fifth try, and came alongside the log raft and I got in. George had to stay with the logs and wait for the tug. We wouldn't get paid until we delivered those logs to the mill, so we couldn't take chances . . . we had a whole winter's work into those logs. When we took off, I could look down and see George working on the lines that kept the log raft tied in the cove, keeping 'em from chafing. He said he'd hitch a ride in with the tug and see me in town.

"It blew like hell that whole night I was in the hospital, and all I could think about was them logs and George and that raft in that cove. I had a little boy, right in the middle of the worst of it.

"George came in the next morning, and right off when I saw his face I knew something had happened.

" 'The raft's gone,' he said. 'I thought we could make it. We got about halfway across, then the chains busted . . . those logs are scattered up and down the strait now.'

"That whole winter's work, gone just like that. The nurse gave him the little boy then, and he asked me what I thought up for a name.

" 'Stormy,' I said. I knew right off without thinking . . . we'd name him for the night he came into the world and when all them logs was lost."

—A friend

The woods and the sea—in no other place in North America are the two as intertwined in the lives of the inhabitants as they are along the coast of Southeast Alaska.

Stormy's mom and dad lived in a home built on a raft of floating logs in a cove away from town. In the winter they would trap in the woods for beaver, living for long periods in tiny shacks dotted along the watersheds of Prince of Wales Island. Sometimes, after Stormy came along, his mom would hunt with him in a backpack. Once, she tracked a wounded deer for most of a day, deeper and deeper into the forest. When she had found and skinned it, she shifted the child around to her front, put the meat on her back, and walked through the night to their home. In the summer the couple would take their small gill-net boat up a remote slough near the British Columbia border. They would haul a log-float and cabin off the beach, tie it between two islands, and live out of it during the salmon season.

Living in a home on a log raft was rarely dull. When it was rainy she might send the kids to fish through the seat in the outhouse into the clear salt water below. Problems could develop that a land person would never encounter.

"We kept smelling propane around our float home, and finally George tracked it down to the propane tank: you know, one of those hundred-pound cylinders. Well, he tried to tighten it, but it just started leaking worse, and we had a wood stove inside and all, plus the smoker going, and we were just afraid that the whole thing was going to catch on fire. So he just unhooked it and rolled it into the bay, let it start drifting out with the tide. George just figured he'd let 'er float out a ways and then sink it with a shot from his rifle.

"This was something different to watch, course, so I was out there with the kids, watching. But then his first shot, it knocked the valve off that sucker, and with all that gas shooting out of it, it started heading right back at us, just like a goddamned torpedo! If it had ever hit the raft at the speed it was going, it would probably have blown up and we all would have been goners! We got a port-hole set into our door, and he got up there and rested his rifle in it to get a better shot. But that darned propane bottle, it wasn't making it very easy for him. Every time he got a good bead on it, it'd take a dive and plow under water for ten or twenty yards before surfacing, still headed right for us. When he finally got it, on the third shot,

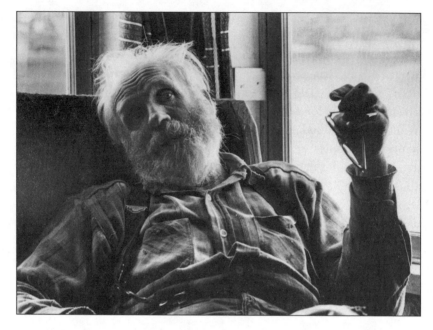

The author's neighbor and friend, Flea, was one of the handful of residents living around Point Baker in 1974.

he blew a hole right in its side, sent it spinning before it finally sank, but for a while there, I was sure we were goners."

—A friend

Today the infant she carried works in a log-sorting yard forty miles away on the other side of the island. His mother works as a flagger on the logging roads that crisscross the land. She has no phone for direct communication with her son and new granddaughter, but occasionally a driver of one of the huge log trucks will toot his horn, slow, and point to a message spray-painted on the rough sides of the logs: "Hi Mom, Annie got her first tooth, hope you're O.K. Love, Stormy."

When Vancouver explored this area of Clarence Strait, which is the wide channel north from Ketchikan, it was late in his second season of exploration. He had traveled almost a thousand miles with his two ships and many more in the small boats since entering the Juan de Fuca Strait the previous June. If he was discouraged, he didn't say so.

Here and in most of Southeast Alaska, the peaks that define the boundary with Canada form a dramatic snowy wall in the east. In the mornings, the mountains, shining and cold, loom above the land along the coast. It would be hard for an explorer to see these and think there might be a path through. Yet Vancouver continued north, drafting his chart with remarkable accuracy. He must have been an unusually talented seaman, or unusually lucky, for his journey became a series of close calls with stormy weather, poor visibility, and rocky shores.

Vancouver's crews' relations with the natives seemed to be deteriorating. On August 12, in a place he named Traitors Cove, twenty-five miles north of what is now Ketchikan, Vancouver and his party were attacked. Only Lieutenant Swaine's timely arrival in the launch and his firing a volley of pistol shot into the natives saved the situation. The natives fled, but the incident was a reason for alarm. Vancouver speculated that white traders had begun to show up on the coast, and that they were giving inferior goods for the highly valued sea otter pelts.

> And I am extremely concerned to be compelled to state here, that many of the traders from the civilised world have not only pursued a line of conduct, diametrically opposite to the true principles of justice in their commercial dealings, but have fomented discords, and stirred up contentions, between the different tribes, in order to increase the demand for these destructive engines. They have been likewise eager to instruct the natives in the use of European arms of all descriptions, and have shewn by their own example, that they consider gain as the only object of pursuit; and whether this be acquired by fair and honorable means, or otherwise, so long as the advantage is secured, the manner how it is obtained seems to have been, with too many of them, but a very secondary consideration.
>
> —Vancouver, *A Voyage of Discovery*

CLARENCE STRAIT.   On February 1971, I traveled up Clarence Strait in a new, 108-foot, steel king-crab boat. The vast clear-cuts in the Tongass National Forest that would so change the face of the land within a decade or so were still for the most part hidden behind the hills. We traveled the entire strait without seeing another boat, and so

I suppose what we saw, except for the snow, was little different from what Vancouver had seen.

The morning was still. We'd passed Ketchikan in the night, and first light came to us in lower Clarence Strait. A thin, cold, low, winter light shafted across the cold and snow-covered land from the border peaks. All day we steamed north between forested and snow-covered shores. If there was any life on the land we passed, we couldn't see it.

In the early northern dusk we came to Wrangell Narrows. There the channel winds for twenty miles between two islands, in places barely a stone's throw wide. Part way through, we passed a log cabin, its windows lit both from within and from the pastel sky above. Smoke from the chimney rose into still air. Snow lay deep around it, a graceful little wooden vessel at a mooring before it.

The rest of our trip north was terrible. We were bound for the ice pack, the winter fishery in the desolate reaches of the Bering Sea, far to the west and north on the edge of Siberia. The bitter cold froze the spray instantly to our hull, making us dangerously top-heavy with ice. What should have taken a week stretched into a month.

The Bering Sea was a windy wasteland, on whose shores there were few trees, settlements, or shelter for boats. The wind blew the cups off the anemometer; the ice chewed the paint off our hull.

But in 1971, the Bering Sea king crab fishery was the equivalent of the gold rush. Deep beneath the stormy surface, a vast herd of king crab, spidery creatures with leg span of perhaps six feet, roamed. We fished with pots the size of a small room, seven by seven by three feet. In some places we had our pots as close together as we could place them without tangling the buoy lines. Fishing around the clock and pulling each trap every day and a half, we would bring up pots so full the meshes were bulging, some containing a ton of legal-size crab. It was apparent that the herd of crab on the bottom was several feet thick. Fishing was simply a contest of how long the crew could stay awake.

We began our season on the edge of the ice pack, fishing two or three weeks at a time without seeing another boat. We ended it crowded in with the rest of the fleet, off the turbulent mouths of the passes between the North Pacific Ocean and the Bering Sea.

All that time, fishing off that treeless, bleak, and windy shore, the memory of the log cabin seen in Clarence Strait in winter dusk stayed with me. When the season was over and the opportunity presented itself, I bought a 32-foot salmon gill-net boat and made plans to return to the forested island wilderness of Southeast Alaska.

I came by chance to the roadless settlement of Port Protection on the northern tip of Prince of Wales Island in June of 1972. "Port P," the locals call the place. This is the anchorage Vancouver found when he desperately needed it on Sunday evening, September 8, 1793. His two ships had been exploring the north side of Sumner Strait, making sure they missed no navigable channel. A storm had been threatening from the south all day long, and the ships crossed to the southern shore to try to anchor. But the water was deep right up to the beach, and the ships couldn't anchor; with the light failing, they faced the prospect of a difficult night. At dusk, Lieutenant Broughton in the *Chatham* passed Point Baker, where the shore turns sharply from west to southwest, and he signaled Vancouver that he had found what appeared to be an anchorage.

> We had scarcely furled the sails, when the wind shifting to the south-east, the threatened storm from that quarter, began to blow, and continued with increasing violence during the whole night; we had, however, very providentially reached an anchorage that completely sheltered us from its fury, and most probably from imminent danger, if not from total destruction. Grateful for such an asylum, I named it Port Protection.
>
> —Vancouver, *A Voyage of Discovery*

Near Port Protection, Susanna and I built a cabin looking out on Sumner Strait. The tide runs hard there, filling any still night with its distant roar. When the wind blew and the trees swayed and creaked around the cabin, I'd look out our window at the churning strait and the wild and unpeopled land beyond. I would imagine Vancouver and his men sailing those cumbersome ships on that evening 180 years before, passing just off our cabin site anxiously seeking shelter.

Or I would think of all the ships that had carried the herd of humanity to the Klondike: the *Valencia* and the *Cottage City*, the *Clara Nevada* and the *Al-Ki*, the *Islander*, the *Yucatan*, the *City of Seattle*, and dozens of others.

In the black distance, winking as it bobbed up and down in the swell pushing up the strait from the ocean, was the buoy that marked Mariposa Reef. Here, on a November night in 1917, Captain Johnny O'Brien napped in his cabin, his vessel steered by a pilot. Sumner Strait runs like a river, and the swift currents carried the fast and beautifully appointed liner, *Mariposa*, onto the rocks, where she remained.

Ghosts passed before me. The three-master, *Star of Bengal,* was towed past Point Baker in September 1920 behind two tugs. Before they reached the open sea where they would free her for the trip to San Francisco, a storm drove in from the gulf. The tugs cut the big bark loose and ran for shelter. At Helm Point, a thousand-foot sheer cliff on the south side of Coronation Island, the sea became the grave for 111 out of the 132 aboard.

When we had come there, the settlements at Port Protection and Point Baker, two miles apart, formed a community of perhaps sixty people. They created an Alaska very different from the towns where the sawmills and the canneries were. Settlements like these were reached only by boat and float plane. They were communities unto themselves, isolated from the bustle of the larger towns. There was no telephone, no central power or water, no school.

In 1972 these two places had something few other spots in Southeast Alaska had: a piece of land a person could buy. Almost all the land was part of the Tongass National Forest; little was available for settlers. Before the discovery of oil in Prudhoe Bay, when Alaska was a slower-paced place, the forest service, which administers the Tongass National Forest, had a more casual approach to squatters on government land. But the oil rush and the seventies brought people seeking their own little piece of the wilderness, and the forest service, faced with an increasing number of illegal squatters, had little choice but to enforce the law.

Fortunately, the forest service had established a policy of opening for further settlement places around existing communities. In a few sheltered coves, of which Port Protection was one, a person could lease a building lot for a nominal fee.

One of the new families was a young couple from Chicago. They came because they heard land was available; they leased a piece and began to clear it. They were city folk, their woods skills little developed,

Leaky walls and crooked windows didn't diminish the prize possession of this Port Protection cabin— a commanding view of Sumner Strait and Wooden Wheel Cove.

and they became the butt of jokes for doing things like leaving their chain saw on the beach and wondering where it was when the tide came up. The locals had built their homes on the beach or close enough to it for good access. They thought the newcomers foolish for trying to build on a site so high they'd had to construct a cable tramway from the beach to haul up supplies.

One October day, when our fishing season was done, I visited their home site. The lot was a stubby peninsula, dividing the outer bay from the sheltered cove. It was thickly wooded and rose to a ridge perhaps sixty feet up from the water. They had chosen the top of the ridge to build on, a crest, falling away to the water on both sides. They had completed the platform, the plywood base on which their house would be erected. Enough of the great spruces and hemlocks had been felled to frame dramatic views of the water. It was cool the day we visited, and our breath hung in the air before us. The first frost of the fall lay on the yellowish plywood and the fallen trees that surrounded us.

It was a magic place. The broad plywood floor seemed the size of a dance hall, and it commanded a dramatic view of Sumner Strait to the north and west and of Wooden Wheel Cove, the cabins, the boats, and the community to the south and east. Our new friends described how they were going to build, where the windows and the door would be. I barely listened, wandering back and forth across the plywood in awe of what they were doing. No matter what others thought for building up there, it was a hauntingly beautiful place for a home.

The following spring, the house was up. At first they had tried to build a stockade-style log home from the dozens of huge trees that lay felled like pickup sticks all around the house site. The logs, so heavy they had to be jacked and winched in place, kept falling over. Finally they ordered a load of timbers to be sent out on the mail boat from the sawmill in Wrangell, forty-two miles east. The mail boat lowered the timbers into the water. They floated them to the beach and hauled them up a few at a time on the pulleys of the gasoline-powered tramway.

Then they built the house, as if with Lincoln Logs, stacking and spiking the timbers together on their sides and cutting out the door and window openings later with a chain saw.

It wasn't perfect. The green timbers, spiked together with little or no caulking, dried and shrank from the heat of the wood stove inside, allowing snow and wind to blow through the cracks. The crudely cut and split cedar shakes that covered the exterior walls ran in drooping lines. The bottom of the stairs ended in a wall, without room for a landing. The wood stove leaked; the inside of the house smelled of creosote and stale food.

The house was something settlers a hundred years before might have put together. But for those new Alaskans, it was a remarkable achievement, although it hadn't been without a price. As temporary quarters they had constructed a tiny, perhaps eight-by-ten, windowless cabin in the thick woods. The winter there had been dark, gloomy, and extremely long. In the fall, my friend's wife had been cheery, outgoing. In the spring, she seemed almost catatonically depressed; it took her years to recover.

My own cabin was a simple twelve-by-sixteen frame affair with a covered back porch and a sleeping loft. It came down to what was the least expensive structure that we would live in. We got our windows and doors at Seattle garage sales and prefabricated the kitchen counter, sink, and drawers. Friends hauled the pieces of our new life north on their fish packers. We took the rest aboard our own boat and headed north, towing a skiff laden with all the odds and ends needed to build a cabin. It was May 1973.

Early every morning we'd take our little outboard from the dock at Point Baker and motor through the twisting back channel between the cabins of our neighbors. We'd come around the corner into our cove and look with awe at the little home we were creating.

When it was done, we walked around it in wonder. Sumner Strait was out the front, Mount Calder and the channel to Port P out the back. We put our sleeping bags in the loft and made driftwood furniture.

It was a tiny house, little more than a shack. Yet even that small project impressed me with the difficulty of getting anything done in the wilderness, so far from the nearest store. Every time I visited my friend's house on the point, I was amazed at the dimension of what they had taken on, flawed though it was.

In the early 1970s, forest service leases were running around twelve hundred dollars a year, and there was a good possibility that the lessees would eventually be able to buy their leased land at very reasonable prices. And not only was there land, there was good fishing close at hand.

Most of the newcomers took up hand trolling, towing arrays of salmon baits, plugs, and spoons through the water, cranking the fish aboard with little winches called hand gurdies. The small vessels that fished this way were baby brothers to the power trollers, larger vessels that fished four lines they hauled up by engine power.

Most fishing boats in the region have at least modest quarters and a stove of some sort, for most of the fisheries involve a stay of days or weeks away from town. But many of the young settlers in places like Port Protection could only afford open skiffs, puddle jumpers as they were known locally. A Briggs & Stratton air-cooled engine was connected to the propeller shaft with an arrangement of belts and pulleys to provide affordable propulsion. When the fishing wasn't good at Baker, these men packed up their gear, and sometimes their families, and tented, following the fish up and down the coast.

This was an echo of the past, of the twenties and thirties, when hand trollers fished and traveled in fleets, setting up tent cities on remote islands and following the fish. Often far from the nearest settlement, they depended on fish-buying vessels for gas and supplies.

In those days, many fishermen couldn't afford engines of any kind, and they worked their boats with long oars which they employed by standing up and facing forward.

> "Sure, for you boys in your big power boats, you don't think nothing of going down to Noyes Island, or up to Icy Strait, if you get a tip that's where the fish are . . . jes set the auto pilot, get a cup of coffee, put yer feet up and enjoy the ride, cruising along at ten, eleven knots. You ought to take a trip down with us, taking every long cut we can to get out of the weather, going along at six knots, standing out there in your oilskins with no toasty oil stove to belly up to. You ought to try finding some place to beach yer skiff and set up your tent and get some hot grub in ya some evening with the rain pouring down, after y' been fishing since maybe four or five that morning."
>
> —A friend

In an average to better year, a good hand troller working out of Point Baker, home in his own bed every night, might be able to catch six or eight thousand dollars worth of fish.

Fishing was pretty much done by the first of October, and money was hard to come by after that. Trolling for kings was still open, but those winter kings were generally few and far between. If a guy hadn't made his season in the summer, the long dark months between October and April could be pretty hard. A person could always go into town (Wrangell or Ketchikan) for the winter and work in the pulp mills or sawmills, but trapping was about the only other local alternative for money.

> "We ended up trapping for most of the winter. Most of the good trapping territory around Port P was pretty much already taken, so we ended up quite a ways away. That meant we had to live in the little

Packing their families with them, small hand trollers often followed the fish, sometimes earning $8,000 in a season.

bow-picker [a 26-foot gill-net boat], instead of our little cabin. Luckily there were plenty of minks and martens where we ended up, but it was a cold old winter, and that bow-picker wasn't really set up for it.

"We didn't have a diesel stove, just the little propane cooker, so it was always cold. The worst of it was that the walls weren't insulated, so after we turned the stove off and went to bed at night, all that moisture would condense on the walls and freeze. It didn't bother John too much, he's got short hair, but about every other morning, I'd wake up and my hair would be froze to the wall. I couldn't even move until John got up, heated up some water, and melted the ice. I didn't mind the rest of it, but that part wasn't much fun."

—A friend

But still, where else in the whole country could you get a piece of land on the water, start building your house, buy a fishing boat, and start making enough money to live on, all for less than five thousand bucks?

Plus, part of the deal with leasing one of the lots from the forest service was that you got to cut 10,000 board feet of lumber free, plenty to build a small house with. In 1977, one of the young settlers brought in a small sawmill powered by a Volkswagen engine and the land rush was on.

The first to be built on were the lots along the shore, followed by those in the second or third row back, where the trees were monsters, six and eight feet in diameter, eighty or a hundred feet to the first branch. The new settlers cut just enough to clear a house site, putting crude plank boardwalks across the boggy places.

To walk among the back lots in the mid and late 1970s was like stepping back in time: crude plank houses were taking shape among the dark forest giants, with the wood smoke rising into the dripping canopy above. They looked like the photographs of early settlements in Alaska, Washington, and Oregon.

Most of the older folks more or less welcomed the younger fishermen to the community and shared with them their experience and their knowledge of the fisheries. A few resented the newcomers.

"That first spring I started out halibut fishing out of my skiff. It was just a 16-footer with a Briggs & Stratton for power, and I only had three skates of gear. [A skate is a unit of halibut gear, usually a hundred hooks, 600 feet of line, and a buoy and anchor at each end.] I tried to go out where there wasn't any other gear set, you know, so I wouldn't step on anyone's toes, being a newcomer and all, but I kept losing gear. I'd set out my gear, come back the next day, and it wouldn't be there. At first I thought it might be the tide sweeping the buoys under, so I went out at slack water looking, but still, no buoys. I was wild, the only thing I could figure was that someone was cutting me off, that they didn't want me fishing there.

"So finally I took my rifle out with me and camped on my gear; I put up a tent in woods, where I could look out and see my buoy. I hid the tent pretty well, and took my skiff way up around a bend in the creek, so you'd never see it from the salt water, and just waited. Sure enough, just at first light the next morning, this boat came around the point and stopped right by my buoy. I'd set so that the buoy was pretty close to the shore, so he wasn't more than fifty yards from where I was hiding in the woods. I'd already sighted in my rifle on the buoy the night before. The guy grabbed a gaff hook, and he was just getting ready to pick up my buoy, and I put a shot into the water about ten feet off his stern. That was all it took. He looked around, real surprised like, and put his gaff slowly back on the deck. You know, I'd see the guy around town sometimes, and he'd nod to me like everyone else, but I didn't have no trouble after that."

—A friend

A few hundred yards away from our cabin was the place where the tidal currents boil as Sumner Strait turns a sharp corner. These eddies churned plankton to the surface and were a favorite spot for humpback whales in the summer. On a still evening, when there was no wind to rustle the trees around our cabin, you could clearly hear the whales blowing as they surfaced after a few minutes under water.

The eddies were a popular fishing spot, where I suggested my parents go to catch a salmon when they visited one summer. My skiff that year was a typical puddle jumper, powered with a Briggs & Stratton engine. It ran well, but I hadn't finished installing the controls, so the speed could only be controlled by turning a screw in and out on the carburetor. I started the engine for them, and sent them out to the tide rip, while I remained at our net float, working on gear. "Oh yeah," I said as they departed, "there's a bunch of whales that fool around in that tide rip, but they shouldn't bother you."

A little later I heard what sounded like screams and looked out to see my parents and the skiff more or less surrounded by a pod of whales, coming up all around them. When they finally made it back to the float they were pale from their experience. The engine had stopped, and before they could get it restarted, the whales were playing all around them; what had looked fascinating from a distance was terrifying up close.

Although our cabin was on a secluded cove, it was only a ten-minute skiff ride from neighbors and the settlement at Point Baker. At night the darkness was broken only by the flashing light at West Rock, where Sumner Strait turns the corner.

In the summer, cruise ships would pass, floating cities like the 400-foot *Spirit of London*. They'd come around the point, filling up the darkness with light and the odd, out-of-place noise of music and voices.

Mail Day lures the scattered inhabitants of Point Baker and Port Protection. In the 1970s, many young people moved to these rugged communities, where scenery compensated for lack of phones, power, and running water.

They'd pass beyond the other point, and there would be only the dark and the sigh of the wind or the rush of the tide.

Just inside the harbor entrance at Point Baker was a bar and general store built on a log raft, with plenty of room for vessels to tie up. In this fashion, the nasty problem of having to negotiate a steep and slippery ramp down to one's boat after having a few drinks was avoided. The Point Baker floating bar was the closest drinking spot to good fishing grounds in all of Alaska. Of course, for people used to more urban bars, like myself in 1972, the Point Baker floating bar took a little getting used to. We tied up there after an eight- or ten-day trip from Seattle; I thought I'd stand the couple on the boat traveling with us, our "running partner" for the trip, to a round of drinks.

The bartender turned from the rough-looking fellows at the other stools and came over to us.

"What'll it be, fellas?"

"Let's see," Susanna said, "maybe I'll have a stinger. How 'bout you, Joe, want your usual rum and tonic?"

"Look here, pals," the bartender replied, "we got whiskey and water, whiskey and Coke, and whiskey and Tang. What's it gonna be?"

The cook in the back occasionally wore boots. As time passed and the logs became waterlogged, the building would ride a little lower in the water, and on a busy night with a lot of customers aboard he might be ankle-deep in salt water.

Behind the building that housed the bar lay the 60-foot tug and onetime fish-buying vessel *Dividend*, which the owners used to transport supplies out from Petersburg. The walls and floors of the fish hold were carpeted, because the vessel had served as their home until they were able to move into more roomy quarters ashore. One summer, when there was an unexpectedly large run of fish in the area and a shortage of fish packers, the *Dividend* was pressed into service, carpeting and all.

"Yeah," the owner laughed later, "those were probably the first fish in Alaska to go to town in a *carpeted fish hold!*"

It may be no surprise that a bar so close to good fishing attracts its own sort of people. One rainy night, I had tied to the float to sleep for a few hours before going out to make the daylight set with my gill net. Before I hit the bunk, though, I put on my rain gear and stepped out onto the float to take the dog for a walk. The dimly lighted windows of the bar provided but the faintest visibility, and as I walked past what I thought was a bundle of trash on the dock, a hand reached up and grabbed my leg. I stopped, startled, and looked down. Another hand reached up to me with a pint bottle of whiskey.

"Hey, young fellow," a throaty, rasping voice called out, "care for a snort?"

I recognized the prone shape as one of our senior local fishermen, who was taking a little rest on the float before he got into his skiff to row off in the dark to his cabin. It was an awful mean night, so I took him up on his kind offer.

Most people in these remote communities were there because they liked it the way it was. When the forest service announced a plan to expand the network of logging roads to serve Port P and Point Baker, it stirred up a hornet's nest of opposition. Alerted by the residents, national environmental organizations got involved.

The most vocal opponent of the proposed roads was a young man whose skiff we had taken to calling the Widow-Maker. In Southeast, a widow-maker is a logger's term for a dangerously leaning tree or an overhanging branch that could fall on a careless or unlucky logger. In this case, it was the young man's Boston Whaler, which was dangerously overpowered with a very high horsepower Mercury outboard he had hung on it, and doubly dangerous for the way the controls were set up, or not set up. You steered with the steering wheel in the middle seat, but the engine controls were not connected there, so the engine could only be controlled from the stern. What this Port P resident usually did was point the boat straight, start the engine, get it going full speed, say forty knots, and then clamber over the seat to the steering station as the craft was pounding over the choppy bay. Also, because the Boston Whaler is basically unsinkable, and because it rains a great deal in Southeast Alaska, he usually left the boat at the dock with the drain plug out, so the water would seek its own level and flow out the plug whenever he used the boat. As everyone in the community basically wore knee-high rubber boots, or "Alaska tennis shoes," when they were out and about, having four or five inches of water in one's skiff wasn't a problem.

One afternoon I happened to be on the dock when a chartered float plane arrived with representatives of both the National Audubon Society and the Sierra Club, dressed in city clothes. They seemed taken aback when they realized their ride to the next bay, where the locals were trying to stop the siting of a logging camp, was the Widow-Maker. They came back paler still. Later I got the story of their skiff ride across the bay.

"I was just trolling along off the mouth of the back channel when I sees the Widow-Maker screaming through with these two dudes all dressed up in city slicker clothes fer passengers, lookin' scared out of their wits and holding on fer all they was worth. They got about halfway across, and all of a sudden the driver sees a bunch of ducks starting to get off the water ahead. He always kept a shotgun aboard, like we all do, but because of where those controls were and everything, he knew that if he took the time to get back to the controls and slow down, those ducks would have been history. So he just grabbed the shotgun, let go of the steering wheel, stood up and started blasting away at the ducks, and them clipping along full bore. Man, I didn't know who those dudes were, but even I could tell that they weren't really ready for *that!*"

—A friend

The story may or may not be true, but it gives a sense of the gulf of perception and understanding that sometimes existed between the people of the outport communities and the people on the outside who became involved in their affairs.

In the summer, most of my neighbors and I were busy fishing. Sometimes we'd be gone from Baker for weeks or months at a time, following the fish up and down the coast. It was in the fall and winter that we had time to visit.

The woods were so thick that even to visit a neighbor, most people used their skiffs. Many of our friends were in Port Protection, which we reached via a winding and rocky channel. On one November visit, we stayed later than anticipated. What had begun as an impromptu visit became a full-fledged dinner party—two chickens went to the block— and our friend, a colorful tugboat operator turned gill-netter, showed us around his place. Over the previous winter he had constructed a big barn and filled it with his possessions, which previously he had stashed here and there all over Southeast Alaska. The whole building was filled with . . . stuff. Old engines, old nets, pieces of boats, boxes of magazines, broken furniture. Our friend walked us through it and proudly waved around at the incredible collection.

"And it's all here by *choice!*"

When we stepped outside to head home, the night was cloudless and extremely dark. A mist lay on the surface of the bay, through which we made our way.

I had forgotten the compass so we navigated by sound. Two of the families had little generators popping away, making electricity for their freezers and lights. We'd travel a few minutes, then shut off our outboard and listen to orient ourselves. When the sound of the generators became faint and finally died away to nothing, it would be the sea, washing softly on the rocks of the shore, that we'd listen for.

When we came to the back channel, the tide was extremely low.

Parts of the channel were wide enough for two boats to pass at high tide but barely wide enough for our skiff at low tide. At night, by flashlight, with kelp-draped rocks looming unnaturally large all around us, it seemed totally unfamiliar. For part of it we had to shut off the outboard, tilt it up, and push ourselves through, the water was so thin.

"You know where we are?" Susanna's question only reinforced my doubts. The channel which I thought I knew so well suddenly seemed not familiar at all. We stopped again and again for a long listen, for we should have been near some of the other houses at Point Baker; I hoped to see a light, hear the sound of a generator. But it was late, the generators probably shut down, and there was only the distant rush of the tide in the strait, and the wet sounds of rain in the woods close at hand.

Then we heard our dog barking, and we followed the channel until our flashlight revealed the slippery rock bank below our cabin, and we were home.

THE BUSH PLANE.   Point Baker wasn't the bush pilot's favorite destination. The entrance to the harbor was a slot between two thickly wooded islands, and the harbor itself was barely long enough to land in. Normally, in a place like that the pilot would land the plane in the wider waters outside, where he had plenty of room, and taxi in to his destination. At Point Baker, however, the tide rips that frequently boiled up outside the harbor entrance made that riskier than landing inside the harbor. Fog was a problem, too. In 1975, a twin-engine float plane, either trying to find Point Baker in the fog or trying to set down on the water to wait for the fog to lift, crashed a mile outside the harbor. The trollers who were working in the area at the time heard the plane's engines and then heard the impact and a horrifying silence. When they searched, they found only bits and pieces of the plane: no survivors.

A similar fate met a single-engine plane taking off from Point Baker a decade earlier. Whether the plane caught a gust and sideswiped a tree in the entrance, or entered the tide rips before it could get airborne, will never be known; the result was the same: the plane and all in it were lost.

On a windy afternoon in December 1973, my wife and I waited for

Landing an airplane can be a bracing adventure at Point Baker, where the constricted waters of the harbor are often the only reliable place to set down.

a plane at the float at Point Baker. We were going south for a few months, and we had a lot of luggage. As the pilot circled overhead, looking at the pattern the wind made on the water of the harbor, a friend showed up. He wanted to get a ride out with us.

As the plane settled into our narrow strip of water, you could tell the pilot was struggling with the wind, which was tossing the airplane back and forth. He put it down hard and taxied over to the float. After tying up, he surveyed all our gear.

"If I'd known you had this much stuff," he said somewhat anxiously, "I'd have brought the Beaver." The Beaver is a larger, more powerful airplane than the Cessna 185 he had flown in.

I shrugged. I hadn't known about my friend and how much luggage he had.

The pilot walked around our pile of gear again, then strode to the end of the float from which one could see the big tide rip boiling in five-foot combers just outside the harbor mouth. It was an extremely sobering sight.

After we'd gotten into the airplane, I looked down at the floats; they were almost awash. If we weren't over our legal maximum weight, we were right on it. My heart began to rise in my throat as the pilot slowly taxied up to the very head of the harbor, threading his way between the rocks to get the longest possible takeoff run.

No one said anything; we were all aware of what lay outside the harbor; tension was heavy in the air.

Finally, the pilot finished his checklist and pulled the throttle out. The engine roared, the tail squatted down, but the plane moved slowly; we were *very* heavy. When 200 yards had passed without the plane really getting up on top of the water, fear was like a cold stone in my chest. I was seated in the right-hand seat, next to the pilot, and I started to lean over to ask him to abort. Then there was no more time. The narrow exit between the trees was ahead; we were committed, though we were still way below takeoff speed with the load we carried. We rushed through the gap, still struggling to get into the air. The pilot pulled back on the wheel and we staggered a foot or two into the air before settling heavily back onto the increasingly choppy water. He let us bang heavily along for another twenty-five or thirty yards and pulled the wheel back again—we had run out of room. The plane groaned as it lifted prematurely into the air; the steep breaking seas of the rip rushed by barely a couple of feet beneath our floats.

The airplane started to settle; we all felt it. I lifted my feet without realizing it, as if that would help. The pilot pulled the wheel gently back, treading ever so carefully the path between stalling the plane and clipping a wave top with a float. The result of either would be the same.

For a single timeless moment we skimmed, perhaps inches from burying a float, tripping, and crashing into the sea. And then the moment was over. We gathered a few more knots of airspeed, rose from the sea and were on our way.

I thought the bad part was over, but we hadn't made a third of the distance to Ketchikan before the snow started and the visibility began dropping. Our comfortable cruising altitude of 800 feet dropped until we had barely thirty feet, and the pilot throttled back. Every now and then the dark shape of an island or a headland would flash by, to be glimpsed for a moment in the gloom and snow and then be gone. I worried about encountering a tug or a big fish packer. In the reduced visibility and at the height we were flying, I wasn't sure we'd clear the rigging. Then, finally, when it seemed as if the snow was coming on harder and daylight was failing, the familiar shape of the lighthouse at the Guard Islands rushed by our wing tip. A few minutes later we settled heavily onto the choppy channel in Ketchikan and taxied over to the float. When our gear had been unloaded, I spoke to the pilot.

"Well, what d'ya think of that takeoff outa' Baker? I mean, was that no big deal, or did we come pretty close to taking a bath?"

The pilot looked at me for a moment and then out at the channel. The snow eddied around us. The ceiling by now had dropped right down to the water, and visibility was less than a hundred feet. If we'd been ten minutes later in getting out of Baker, we'd have been forced down by the snow, maybe to land in one of the coves off Clarence Strait, to wait until morning.

"Close one." That's all he said.

PETERSBURG AND WRANGELL NARROWS.   In 1793, Wrangell Narrows was a muddy slough; Vancouver's men spent little time there. Today it is a dredged channel and the main route north, used by Alaska state ferries and the smaller cruise ships as well as thousands of fishing vessels every season.

Vessels too large for this twenty-mile shortcut between Sumner Strait and Frederick Sound are forced to dogleg around Kupreanof and Kuiu islands, a distance of almost 150 miles.

By day, passage through the winding narrows is one of the most dramatic phases of the voyage. The channel, especially the southern part, seems like a small river issuing from the forest, rather than a major saltwater thoroughfare. By night, the seventy-odd red, green, and white flashing lights at the tightest parts of the passage make it look more like a video game than a part of the Alaskan wilderness.

But it is the fog that truly challenges mariners here. Many vessels simply anchor and wait for clear weather to avoid facing it.

A radar screen shows only shapes; the interpretation is up to you. A buoy, a 30-foot boat, and a rocky islet may look distressingly similar. Combine this with a swift current that sometimes sweeps obliquely across the channel, and you have the ingredients for vessels to get into trouble.

Fellow travelers usually give wide berth to **Phillips Foss,** *here sailing the Wrangell Narrows while towing a barge load of containers.*

One foggy July night, we approached the narrows in a loaded fish packer after an eighteen-hour steam from Garnet Point at the southern tip of the state. I wanted to anchor, get some sleep, and move in daylight. But the cannery wanted the fish that night, so we proceeded.

A big tide was pushing into the narrows; the current was like a river running in a gorge. To navigate the narrows on such a night, in such a current, requires that you have the chart firmly in memory. The targets move toward you so rapidly on the radar there is little time to consult the chart, study the radar, and steer.

On the screen the channel was an inch wide. This electronic marvel that so many boats rely on cannot discern targets closer than seventy-five feet; they simply merge into the sea clutter in the middle of the screen. On this nighttime run to the cannery in the fog, many markers disappeared into the middle of the screen as we looked ahead anxiously for the lights.

Of the sixty or seventy marker lights we passed, three emerged briefly from the fog right ahead of us as the tide swept us by. The rest were shapes on the radar. Finally, we put on sweatshirts and went out on deck. The crew stood by with the lines while I steered from the flying bridge, the better to feel our way to the crowded wharves at Petersburg.

For a few minutes I steered by the compass, shivering as the cold fog swirled around me. If there was a town to the east of us, there was no sign of it. Then a dim glow appeared ahead. The glow brightened and resolved itself into the dock lights at the Icicle Seafoods cannery and freezer plant complex. It didn't matter that it was two in the morning. The plant was operating around the clock to keep up with a big run of fish.

I swung around into the current to wait as another big packer, already unloaded and high in the water, pulled out of one of the unloading berths and groped off through the fog toward the ice plant. It was our turn.

The tide was running hard, perhaps a four-knot current was swirling under the wharves. We managed to get into our spot without hitting the boats on either side. Barely were the lines around the piling before the cannery's unloading crew was climbing down the ladder, taking off our hatch covers, and guiding the big aluminum vacuum unloader pipe into the fish.

Our engineer went down into the engine room to change the oil and service the machinery. Mary Lou checked over her fish receipts and grocery lists and lay down until the office opened. We had to be unloaded, cleaned up, fueled, full of ice and provisions, and under way again in twenty hours. The quick turnaround in town was the busiest part of the week.

I climbed the long ladder up to the busy dock and walked along the thick planks, dodging fork lifts, to stretch my legs after the long trip. Down a long ramp I went, out onto a float at the north side of the cannery where smaller boats were tied. Out to the very end.

There were no dock lights; it was almost totally dark. The current swirled restlessly around the float and the piles that held it, and I looked for a very long time into the fog and the blackness through which we had come, amazed that we had been able to pick our way through the narrows and find the cannery on such a night.

One of the challenges of operating out of this port is the swift tidal currents that sweep across the face of the wharves. At certain stages of the tide, these currents may reach six knots. Landing calls for a quick hand at the throttle and the crew standing by with the fenders. You like to swing around into the current to make an up-tide landing, and you don't take the engine out of gear until the lines are made fast to the float or to piles.

Smaller vessels generally have enough power for the operator to recover from a poorly planned landing. But for the big tenders and fish packers, perhaps very heavily laden, it can be a different story. At some of the cannery docks where the big boats unload, the current sweeps directly into the dock. In a boat drawing ten or twelve feet of water, loaded with two or three hundred thousand pounds of fish, once you approach the dock with the current behind you, you're committed. And the docks are often so crowded that vessels have to make down-tide landings into spaces a few feet longer than the boat.

Landings get to be a *big deal*. When you blow a landing at Petersburg with a big boat, the results can be spectacular. I recall 1975, when I was operating the ferrocement fish packer *North Wind*. We pushed through the narrows and into cannery row on a rare hot after-noon after a twenty-two-hour steam down from the northern districts. The tide was running hard, and at our cannery the whole shift was taking their break out on the wharf, sitting on the piling with their coffee and cookies. I wanted to be sure I did a good job; I wanted the superintendent to see what a good tenderman he'd gotten in me.

There was a lull on the waterfront just then. Most of the fleet was out, so everyone on the dock was focused on our landing.

I idled the engine back for the approach, but the hot, thin oil in the old tub couldn't make enough pressure in worn bearings to hold off the automatic alarm, and the engine shut itself down. In any other vessel, you'd touch the starter button and be back in business. But the *North Wind*'s creative engine controls presented a dilemma: you couldn't put the engine into neutral from the pilothouse unless the engine was run-ning, and you couldn't start the engine unless it was in neutral.

We struck the piling a glancing blow and I saw coffee and cookies flying, workers scattering like bowling pins along the dock. We whirled off in the current toward the airplane float, where a million dollars worth of float planes, four Cessna 185s and two de Havilland Beavers, lay in our path. I dove into the engine room with hammer and pliers, desperate to get going before we cleaned out the airplanes too.

But the God of War Surplus smiled on us that day; we got started and got back to the cannery with little more than a red face.

At the peak of the salmon season, several hundred gill-netters (30 to 40 feet), fifty seiners (larger), and thirty or so tender ships (60 to 100 feet) might all be operating out of the largest cannery, Icicle Seafoods. Tenders returning from remote fishing districts might have only ten or twelve hours to unload, to take on ice, fuel and groceries, and to make repairs before heading out again.

The trick for tender operators is to use the two or three hours "under the hoist," when they are unloading and tied to the dock, to get all their supplies for the next week. It's easier to load groceries and so forth when you're tied to the dock than when you're fourth or fifth boat out.

The slick part about the Icicle Seafoods cannery is that it's right next to the grocery store. It was great. We would get our groceries, typically two or three full carts, because we were also filling food orders for the smaller boats that fished for us, and we would roll the carts out of the store, down the sidewalk, and onto the cannery dock. The boat could be reached only by climbing down a slippery twenty or thirty-foot steel ladder, so we'd hook onto the cart with the dock hoist (an electrically operated winch) and then *lower the whole full shopping cart right down to the deck of the boat!*

The business of Petersburg is fishing. Its sturdy fishermen with the wind-lashed faces and the Norwegian surnames are known up and down the coast for their skill and endurance.

The quaint appearance of the docks and the fishing fleet at Petersburg belie the fact that some extremely profitable fishing operations are based in this port. In the mid 1970s, a group of young and aggressive Petersburg fishermen who had been brought up in the modestly profitable salmon fisheries of Southeast Alaska expanded their operations into the rapidly growing fisheries of western Alaska, primarily for salmon and herring.

Ten years later, many of these fishermen, by then in their late thirties and early forties, were making six-figure net incomes from fisheries that started in March and were over by the first of August.

The first years were challenging. They would send their boats 2,500

*A retort—or salmon cooker—
in a Petersburg cannery.*

miles from Seattle by barge to the remote, treeless rivers of western Alaska, places with few facilities. They would fly there to fish.

"When we flew up to meet the barge, there was so much ice they couldn't get close to town. We had to take a plane over to the nearest beach, and then get a skiff ride through the ice floes to the barge. Then we had to climb up over four layers of containers to the boat. We just lived up there, fifty feet up in the air, for three or four days while they waited for the ice to push out of the river. Finally we got tired of waiting and had them launch us. It was after dark before we finally got into the water, so we decided to just tie onto the stern of the barge for the night rather than be trying to go somewhere in the black with the tide boiling past and all that ice churning around. There were four or five of us, all trailing behind the barge, and it all went O.K. until the tide turned in the middle of the night, and the ice pushed us under the big sloping bow of the barge and started smashing the antennas and lights off our mast.

"We finally got out of there and went herring fishing. After that there were three weeks to kill before salmon started, so we just wanted to fly home. But back then there wasn't even any place to tie your boat up or haul it out. Finally we just steamed up into the head of a creek at high tide, drove our brand-new boat right up onto the bank, tied it between a bunch of scrub trees and bushes, locked the door and walked to the dirt airstrip, and hoped it'd be there when we got back."

—A friend

Southeast Alaska is rainy country. You can go a whole summer without going out in your T-shirt. The winters are long. In December the sun comes up after nine and is down a little after three. Cabin fever isn't just an expression, but a very real demon that comes out of the woodwork when the days get short.

Yet for all that, it can be a magic place. The grandeur of the land, the sense of wilderness, the woods, and the sea surround you inescapably, even in the towns.

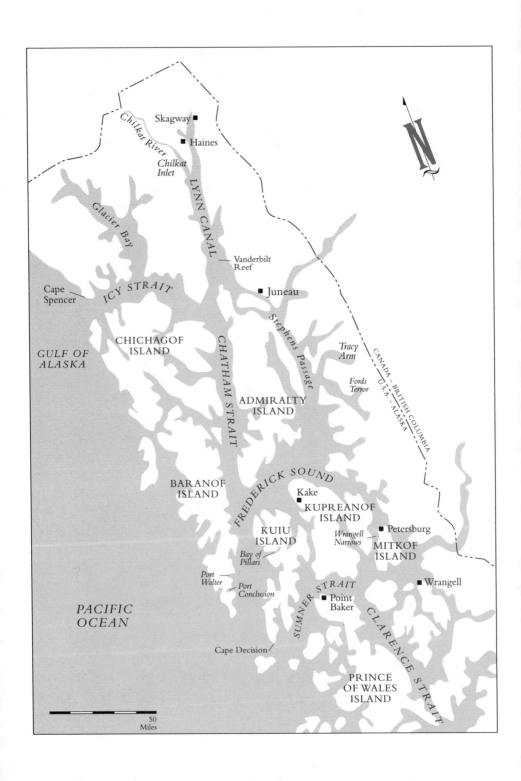

Skagway

Chilkat River

Haines

Chilkat
Inlet

N

LYNN CANAL

Glacier Bay

Vanderbilt
Reef

Cape
Spencer

ICY STRAIT

Juneau

CHICHAGOF
ISLAND

Stephens Passage

CHATHAM STRAIT

Tracy
Arm

GULF OF
ALASKA

Fords
Terror

ADMIRALTY
ISLAND

CANADA – BRITISH COLUMBIA

U.S.A. – ALASKA

BARANOF
ISLAND

FREDERICK SOUND

Kake

KUPREANOF
ISLAND

KUIU
ISLAND

Wrangell
Narrows

Petersburg

MITKOF
ISLAND

Bay of
Pillars

Port
Walter

Port
Conclusion

PACIFIC
OCEAN

SUMNER STRAIT

Point
Baker

Wrangell

CLARENCE STRAIT

Cape Decision

PRINCE
OF WALES
ISLAND

50
Miles

CHAPTER SIX

Where History Lurks

PETERSBURG TO SKAGWAY

"I WAS A KID, maybe seventeen, in my first summer seining up in Southeast. It must have been '54 or '55, I can't remember. We had a couple of days off between fishing periods and we lay in some bay in Chatham Strait. There was a big old cannery, and the skipper took all of us ashore. It was an amazing place, a whole town out there in the middle of nowhere. A couple of windows were broken out but other than that, it looked like the people had just left and never come back. It was all powered by water, you could feel the water rushing through the big pipes under the floor. The guys were all wandering around inside the big canning area. All the equipment was there, these big flat belts coming down from overhead shafts on the ceiling to run every-thing. The skipper took me aside. 'Watch this,' he said, and he went over to where there were a bunch of big valve wheels sticking out of the floor. He grabbed a hold of one of them and started turning it, and all of a sudden, everything in the whole room came to life—all the machines started up, until in just a few seconds, the place was full of noise and even the floor was shaking. Man you should have seen those guys jump . . . it was a good thing no one got their finger whacked off or something."

—A friend

Forty miles west of Petersburg is Chatham Strait, a deep, wide, almost canyonlike channel between Baranof, Kuiu, Admiralty, and Chichagof islands. Many cruise ships are too deep and wide to negotiate Wrangell Narrows and must travel out Sumner Strait to Cape Decision and continue their journey north up Chatham Strait. On the Baranof Island side especially, many narrow bays and inlets penetrate deep into the high, rugged country. The sun comes late to some of these bays and snow may be found in places right down to the water's edge, even in early summer.

Here, more than any other place in the region, may be seen evidence of the entrepreneurial blood that flows so strongly in the veins of Alaskans. Ruins on the shore are stark evidence of ventures that started, boomed, and finally failed. These were whaling stations, fish meal plants, salmon salteries and canneries, mines, mink farms, and fox farms.

Go ashore in any bay; poke around. You'll find old piling rotting on the beach, rusting equipment hidden by devil's-club thorns, and pieces of someone's failed dream.

Some of the older plants were built in a time when the building crew came up from Seattle in the spring, built the cannery and operated it, and returned to Seattle in the fall with the product. The seasonal settlements were villages in themselves, complete with roads, boardwalks, a power plant, mess halls, family housing, and a store.

Imagine the logistics, the financing, the headaches these people endured: putting together a whole town in the wilderness, fifty, sixty, or a hundred years ago.

Sometimes, skiff fishermen trolling for salmon got tired of tenting and set up housekeeping for their families in the abandoned buildings in places like Bay of Pillars, Washington Bay, and Big Port Walter.

Canneries could be seasonal structures, abandoned whenever the fishing industry went into decline. Its bustling community long departed, this deserted building looks out over Washington Bay, Alaska.

Excited perhaps by the grand scenery and the living in the wilderness, they made plans to stay the winter. But when the days got short, when the sun went behind the mountains in October not to be seen again until spring, the sobering reality of the Alaskan winter set in; plans made in the long days of summer changed and they left.

Now, for the most part, the people are gone from these shores, the ruins taken over by the forest.

Many businesses, especially salmon canneries and salteries, were used only during the busy summer season, with a caretaker and his family staying in the wintertime. When the fishing played out or the owners suffered financial reverses, sometimes it was cheaper to just pull the caretaker and abandon the whole thing than to send up a crew to strip it. Whole settlements were abandoned, complete with operating powerhouses, warehouses, and shops full of tools and supplies.

In the spring of 1974, we spent a week trolling for king salmon in lower Chatham Strait. Late each afternoon, we'd anchor off a lifeless settlement and go ashore to walk among the stripped and falling down buildings, silent, yet full of the past.

And each morning, in the palest thin yellow light of dawn, the anchor came aboard and we set out once again into the strait. Our wake arrowed out behind us, and the vastness, the power, and the mystery of that lonely country struck me. The sun came up over the Canadian border peaks far to the east, our lines trailed down into the deep, cold water, and it was just us and our partner boat, alone on a couple hundred miles of shoreline. We hardly saw anyone else. To ice our fish we shoveled snow from the shore of an inlet so steep the high June sun hadn't reached it.

Fishing that vast canyon by day and lying off ruined settlements by night only reinforced the mystical feeling Chatham Strait had come to hold for me.

The fishing wasn't very good that trip, and we gave it up. We steamed half a day north and east, to tie up at the Indian village of Kake in Frederick Sound. We savored the sight of kids and dogs playing in the dusty road and the feel of the brass sun beaming in on us until past ten in the evening instead of going over the mountain early.

The next morning came fair and cloudless. We slept in until six, started up, and headed for Rocky Pass, the tortuous, shallow, little-used channel that winds through the trees down to Sumner Strait and our Point Baker cabin.

Before we entered the pass and let the woods and islands close in around us, we looked back one last time to the west and Chatham Strait, that lonely canyon that had cast such a spell on us. The sun was well up by then, and even from forty miles away, the snow-and-ice flank of Baranof Island loomed above the trees and hills of Kuiu Island. In the pinkish-yellow morning light, it was a brilliant, shining wall, and I was reminded of the journals of the first Western travelers to Tibet and Nepal. Wherever they walked, Everest and her sisters were there towering above them, remote and untouchable.

"You know, if you look at a chart, I suppose it's possible for a guy to take Rocky Pass and think he was going up Wrangell Narrows [a parallel channel between two similar islands, some twenty-five miles farther east], but not too danged likely, especially since the Coast Guard yanked the markers out. Now, with them markers gone, its just a terrible place to try and get through, even when you know it.

"Anyway, we were laying in Kake one time, and here comes this big tug, towing a *big* barge, coming up from the south'ard, from Rocky Pass. I took one look at that rig and thought that must be one hell of a skipper to bring it through there.

"Then the tug hauls up alongside of us, and the skipper steps out of the bridge and hails me.

" 'Say,' he sez, shaking his head and waving toward where he'd come from, 'that Wrangell Narrows ain't *nothing* like the chart.' Then he nodded his head over toward Kake, 'And I thought Petersburg was bigger than this.' "

—A friend

STEPHENS PASSAGE. Stephens Passage on a March night, 1982: I had just come off wheel watch and stepped outside for a moment before heading to my bunk. Idly I looked out and ahead. All was black except for a red glow around our running light.

Then something caught my eye: a glowing shape ahead and just a bit to port, seen only faintly through the thin fog. At first I didn't realize what it was. When I did, I ran forward to the pilothouse and pulled the throttle back to idle, as my surprised engineer peered out ahead.

"Ice," I said, "out there to port, a piece maybe the size of a pickup." I could see him pale, even in the dim light of the compass. "There's probably more out there; we'll just jog along until daylight." I stepped back and settled into the other chair. All of a sudden I wasn't sleepy anymore.

Our radar was broken. We tried the crab lights, the big flood lamps up in the rigging for finding crab pot buoys at night, but they only blinded us—they were reflected back by the fog—and we shut them off.

So we idled along, peering anxiously ahead. Our boat was wood and fifty years old. Our load was 140,000 pounds of herring, a big load, almost too big. A Volkswagen-size piece of ice, hit just right, would do us in. But if we went slow and looked carefully, there was just enough light from the moon above the fog to reveal the ice as pale, ethereal shapes against the black. Now and again, red and green and white running lights would appear out of the fog astern: another herring-laden boat, traveling south by radar. They'd pass and we'd pull in behind them; we'd speed up, travel in their wake, relax. But our vessel was one of the slowest, and eventually the other would pull away and disappear, and we'd slow down again.

Around four in the morning, we noticed a glow in the fog behind us to the north. Soon the whole sky lit up as a beamy steel 120-footer overtook us rapidly, the bank of lights high up on the mast turning night into day.

We had passed through a fleet of bergs the size of outbuildings a little earlier. "Lookit those guys," my engineer said, "whoever's on watch's probably just sitting there, watching the radar and twiddling the autopilot knobs once in a while. With those lights on, I doubt if they can even see beyond their bow. There's plenty of ice out there the radar wouldn't pick up but would be big enough to hole them."

A berg the size of a small house might show only a low, rounded hump above the water, invisible on radar. Hit just right, it would slice them open. With their load, they'd be gone in minutes. Yet up in their cozy pilothouse, with the stereo on and surrounded by modern electronics, they probably thought themselves invincible.

Seventeen years before, when I was a boy working in Alaska for the first time, something woke me in the night as our boat lay anchored near Icy Strait. I sat up in my bunk wondering what it was, and then it came again: a faint but insistent scraping, as if another boat had drifted down on us in the night. I stumbled out onto the deck and saw it, eerily lit by the three-quarter moon: a big berg, moving gently down our port side, pushed by the tide. Its irregularly shaped top was even with my head; I reached out to touch it, to try and retrieve some of the gravel clearly visible within its pale, translucent flank. The gravel had been scraped off a canyon floor hundreds of miles away, ten thousand years before I was born. But the ice was hard, its contours softened by melting. My hand could find no purchase, and after a moment the berg moved away in the tide.

I looked around then to see if more ice had come in. The fleet lay silently around us in the steep-sided cove, big packers like ourselves and

An iceberg floats imposingly along Stephens Passage, representing both a beauty and a danger.

graceful seiners, sleeping beneath their masthead lights. There was only the one berg, now being sucked by the tide toward the head of the cove, where it would stop up the narrow channel that ran between the islands like a plug in a tub.

Outside the point I saw a ghostly armada moving in the seven-knot tide of North Inian Pass: eight or nine little bergs, maybe a thousand tons each, showing as big as medium-size boats above the surface. In the moonlight they seemed to glow as if they were lit from within. I wanted to wake my shipmates, but the tide pushed the bergs around the corner to the west and they were gone.

At Le Conte Glacier, eighteen miles east of Petersburg, the ice reaches the salt water for the first time. But the innocent-looking little pieces that drift in with the tide to the canneries in Wrangell Narrows belie the danger ice holds and the power the ice has had in shaping this part of Alaska.

Fifty miles north of Le Conte Bay, the ice reaches the salt water in Tracy and Endicott arms, deep, winding fjords on the east side of Stephens Passage. To go up these arms, the vegetation thinning, disappearing entirely near their heads, is to travel back in geologic time into menacing basins of raw, glacier-scraped rock, filled with the rush from dozens of waterfalls and the roar of falling ice.

GLACIER BAY. At Glacier Bay the ice shows its grandeur and power. The bay immediately became one of the premier sights of the western hemisphere after John Muir discovered it in 1879.

When Vancouver's men explored this section of the coast in July 1794, they hardly made mention of Glacier Bay, for one startling reason: it didn't exist. They found only a wide indentation in the shore, choked with floating ice and backed by a solid wall of ice. There was so much floating ice they named the place Icy Strait; the men in the boats could hardly get through it.

If the Russians explored this bay during their occupation of the region, we have no record of it; too bad. The next recorded visit to the bay after Vancouver's is not until 1877, ten years after the United States bought Alaska from Russia, and in the intervening years stupendous changes had occurred.

In May of 1877, one C. S. Wood arrived by canoe. By his account, the ice front had retreated forty miles from where Vancouver had seen it. Two years passed before the bay was explored again, this time by a man whose journey there would be one of the peak experiences in his life. The man was John Muir.

Muir was forty-one years old, on his way to becoming the most persuasive advocate of wild places in his time. He was an ardent naturalist and amateur glacier expert. His travels through both the California Sierra and the wilds of Alaska with little more than the clothes on his back and a few bits of food are in contrast with today's well-equipped mountaineering expeditions. He was an unusually gifted writer, able to put into powerful prose the experiences in the North that had so moved him.

On his second trip to Alaska, in 1880, he explored what is now known as Brady Glacier, twenty miles west of Glacier Bay. He and his companion, a dog named Stickeen, were trying to get off the glacier before dark and found themselves trapped on an island of ice surrounded by crevasses. They had jumped downhill across a crevasse to get there, assuming that was the way out. The only avenue of escape was either to jump up across that crevasse, which they had barely made jumping down, or to attempt a seventy-five-foot ice bridge, narrow, drooping, and furthermore, attached to the ice on each side ten feet down the crevasse. Muir chose the bridge. As he chopped steps in the ice down to it, straddled it, and inched his way slowly across, chipping down the knife-edged top so the dog could follow, Stickeen whimpered and cried at the sight. When Muir had made it across, the dog refused to follow.

Finally Muir pretended to go away, calling out to the dog that he must follow, that he could make it if he tried.

> Finally in despair, he hushed his cries, slid his little feet slowly down into my footsteps out on the big sliver, walked slowly and cautiously along the sliver as if holding his breath, while the snow was falling and the wind was moaning and threatening to blow him off. When he arrived at the foot of the slope below me, I was kneeling on the brink ready to assist him in case he should be unable to reach the top. He looked up along the row of notched steps I had made, as if fixing them in his mind, then with a nervous spring he whizzed up and passed me out on to the level ice and ran and cried and barked and rolled about fairly hysterical in the sudden revulsion from the depth of despair to triumphant joy. I tried to catch him and pet him and tell him how good and brave he was, but he would not be caught. He ran round and round, swirling like autumn leaves in an eddy, lay down and rolled head over heels.
>
> —John Muir, *Travels in Alaska*

Guided by the firing of guns and a fire built by their Indian companions, Muir and Stickeen arrived back at their camp.

> Stickeen and I were too tired to eat much, and strange to say, too tired to sleep. Both of us, springing up in the night again and again, fancied we were still on that dreadful ice bridge in the shadow of death.

Nevertheless, we arose next morning in newness of life. Never before had rocks and ice and trees seemed so beautiful and wonderful, even the cold, biting rainstorm that was blowing seemed full of loving kindness, wonderful compensation for all that we had endured, and we sailed down the bay through the gray, driving rain rejoicing.

—Muir, *Travels in Alaska*

It was entirely appropriate that Muir was the first to fully explore and write about Glacier Bay. Filled with an intense desire to learn whatever the wilderness could teach him, wherever he could find it, Muir left in his journals a wealth of geographical information and natural history of the region for those who came after him.

He began his voyage by canoe from Wrangell, Alaska, in the middle of October 1879, a time of year when today's 40- and 50-footers travel cautiously. The youngest member of his crew of native paddlers was a lad named Sitka Charley. He told Muir of a bay full of ice where he had hunted seals with his father; he thought he might be able to show them the way.

But it was late in the season, and even the Indians, experienced boatmen, dreaded parts of the trip, especially the crossing of Frederick Sound to Admiralty Island.

When Muir heard from Charley that there would be no firewood in the bay of ice, he was skeptical. Indeed, none of the other native paddlers, in all their lives of canoe travel throughout the region, had ever seen a place without firewood.

Yet when at last they entered the bay, they found a country so new that trees had not yet begun to sprout. Muir found Vancouver's map (which to that point he had relied upon) to be useless. Even Sitka Charley, on whose advice and direction they had come to the bay, said it had changed so much, that so many new islands had appeared since he had last been there, that they engaged another native, who was then sealing in the bay, to guide them.

Onward they pushed into the amazing bay that had been birthed from the ice almost within the lifetimes of those in the canoe.

Muir was exhilarated at what they had found. He had had a keen interest in glaciers for most of his adult life, and now he was one of the first white men to explore the most dramatic place for viewing active glaciers in all of North America.

Unfortunately the natives didn't share his excitement. They didn't know what to make of Muir, who seemed so excited by what he was finding, and they became reluctant to press ahead with their exploration.

The guide whom they had engaged spoke of snowstorms that had trapped hunters, of canoes crushed in the ice, and of huge bergs rising without warning from the bottom.

Nevertheless, the next day, with the wind behind them, they plunged deep into the heart of the bay.

> Then, setting sail, we were driven wildly up the fiord, as if the storm wind was saying, "Go then, if you will, into my icy chamber; but you shall stay in until I am ready to let you out." All this time sleety rain was falling on the bay, and snow on the mountains; but soon after we landed the sky began to open. The camp was made on a rocky beach near the front of the [Grand] Pacific Glacier, and the canoe was carried beyond the reach of the bergs and the berg waves. The bergs were now crowded in a dense pack against the discharging front, as if the storm wind had determined to make the glacier take back her crystal offspring and keep them at home.
>
> —Muir, *Travels in Alaska*

The bay Muir found in 1879 is very different from the bay of today. Most of the glaciers he then observed have retreated many miles, creating narrow fjords in their wake. Grand Pacific Glacier, for example, had by the early 1980s retreated across the border into British Columbia.

Yet the astonishing part is this: Glacier Bay was created unseen by any eye (or at least unrecorded) between 1794, when Lieutenant Joseph Whidbey explored the north coast of Icy Strait, and the late 1870s when Muir and others explored it. During this eighty-year period, a body of ice thirty-five miles long, six miles wide, and a thousand feet deep disappeared.

Over the same period, the ice twenty-five miles to the west at Taylor Bay was advancing. The Indian burial site Vancouver's men had found there is today buried beneath eight hundred feet of ice. Brady Glacier has advanced eight miles since their visit.

Naturalist John Muir first traveled to Alaska in 1879, and his journals remain stirring invocations of the land's power.

As soon as the word of Muir's discovery got out, the bay became a regular steamer stop.

Many have come since Muir to write about and photograph the bay. Yet it was Muir who, arriving by canoe with frightened native paddlers, first and best described its grand and haunting beauty. In his journal Muir shares the spiritual exhilaration that so filled his heart:

The white, rayless light of morning, seen when I was alone amid the peaks of the California Sierra, had always seemed to me the most telling of all the terrestrial manifestations of God. But here the mountains themselves were made divine, and declared His glory in terms still more impressive. How long we gazed I never knew. The glorious vision passed away in a gradual fading change through a thousand tones of color to pale yellow and white, and then the work of the ice-world went on again in everyday beauty. The green waters of the fiord were filled with sun-spangles; the fleet of icebergs set forth on their voyages with the upspringing breeze; and on the innumerable mirrors and prisms of these bergs, and on those of the shattered crystal walls of the glaciers, common white light and rainbow light began to burn, while the mountains shone in their frosty jewelry, and loomed again in the thin azure in serene terrestrial majesty. We turned and sailed away, joining the outgoing bergs, while "Gloria in Excelsis" still seemed to be sounding all over the white landscape, and our burning hearts were ready for any fate, feeling that, whatever the future might have in store, the treasures we had gained this glorious morning would enrich our lives forever.

—Muir, *Travels in Alaska*

Before their canoe trip was over a few weeks later, they had traveled almost eight hundred miles. Few canoeists would make such a trip today at that time of year.

Today the bay is an extremely busy place, especially in midsummer. The National Park Service restricts access by vessels to reduce the disturbance to the humpback whales that feed there.

Nonetheless, it is still essentially that wild and primeval place Muir described. When the fog closes and the floating cities, the cruise ships, have disappeared into the mists, a traveler in a small boat may experience the emotions Muir so keenly felt.

LYNN CANAL. There are a few places on the Inside Passage, especially in smaller craft, where whoever's awake comes forward to see what lies ahead.

One is Pulteney Point in British Columbia. Another is Cape Spencer, Alaska, the conspicuous headland that marks the boundary between the sheltered waters of the Inside Passage to the south and east and the exposed shores of the Gulf of Alaska to the north and west. The shoreline beyond Spencer is unfriendly, with infrequent harbors far apart and difficult to get into when the wind blows. Crossing the gulf is the worst.

"The thing about it was that them guys shoulda' never been out in the gulf in the first place. Dave had a 60-footer, but all the time he had it he'd been inside, working up and down Southeast. He'd never been out in the gulf in a blow. But it was one of those deals he couldn't do anything about. His cannery sold his charter to an outfit up in Seward, and there it was: to make his boat payments, he had to cross the gulf. Well, luckily we could run with them, and we tried to tell them what it would be like, but I don't think they ever paid much attention. Anyway, we all got out there, too far to go back, and of course she come up southeast, a real rip-snorter. We were both jogging along easy, hoping it wasn't going to get any worse, and all of a sudden Dave came over the radio, almost sobbing: 'Annie's gone . . . Annie's gone . . . a big wave smashed out the galley and she's gone . . . it musta washed her over. Help me, please, oh help me!'

"God, you couldn't have picked a worse night for someone to go over the side: about two in the morning and blowing easy fifty, with a big sea on. Anyway, we got swung around and started looking around with the lights, not that I really expected to be able to do anything. But then he come on again, saying he's found her. Turns out a big cross sea busted out both galley windows and the door latch, so when he came down, the water was just sloshing back and forth in there, and there weren't no sign of Annie so he freaked. Then he came back a little later and found her huddled underneath the table in a big pile of soggy dog food. They'd had a couple of fifty-pound bags that had busted, and she'd just washed up underneath all that doggie food. It was almost funny in a way, but 'course they didn't think so.

"That was the worst of it, and we got into Seward O.K. the day after that. And as soon as they tied up they came over to our boat for a drink. They really needed it . . . all their booze bottles had been busted up coming across, too. They looked real rough. And Annie got in there and looked around and starts shrieking, 'Pictures, your pictures are still up!' She was right wacko until I showed her they were screwed to the wall. They wanted to sell their boat right there to the first guy what came down the dock rather than ever facing that trip across again . . . but I talked them out of it."

—A friend

Still another bad place is near Point Retreat, at the bottom end of Lynn Canal, a long wind tunnel of a fjord east of Glacier Bay.

"Looking up at the big Lynn" is what we always said to ourselves when we finally headed up there in our 30- and 40-foot gill-netters. Of all the places we fished in Southeast Alaska, it was Lynn Canal where we could confidently expect the worst weather. Joined to Chatham Strait to the south, it forms a 225-mile-long channel from the edge of the Yukon to the Pacific Ocean at Cape Decision and Cape Ommaney. It seems to funnel the winds between those two radically different climatic zones. In the fall especially, the big weather systems—arctic highs over the Yukon and Pacific lows in the Gulf of Alaska—battle it out in Lynn Canal. It isn't at all uncommon for it to blow forty or fifty knots from the south for a couple of days, stop for a few hours, and then blow just as hard the other way for another three days.

> We came to a place where the water was covered with boards and stuff. But there wasn't a soul left living to call to us for help.
>
> Seemed like, just standing there at the rail and looking at little boards that had once been a ship and straining our eyes to see folks that wasn't there no more, and then looking at them high mountains along Lynn Canal and thinking we had to go over them and on beyond before we even come to the gold country, quieted us all down. Somehow we didn't feel the same way we'd been feeling on the trip up. That country up there didn't look cordial. It made you feel like cutting out the horseplay and saying a prayer for the fellows who wasn't there no more, and for the rest of us who didn't know what was ahead of us, neither.
>
> —Mckeown, *The Trail Led North*

The speaker was a '98-er, headed up from Seattle to participate in the gold rush. The vessel he was on had stopped to search for survivors from the *Clara Nevada*, blown up with thirty-eight lost from, it was rumored, a poorly stowed case of explosives.

His feelings, of the land making a person somber, are echoed by mariners in lower Lynn Canal. The land changes here, rising from a thin screen of trees at the water's edge to a steep mountain spine. It displays a very different aspect from the land to the south: austere, bleak, unfriendly.

"I'd never even leave the harbor fer south in the fall unless they were calling for good weather. And even then sometimes you get caught. We left Skagway one day, the sun was shining; it was even warm in the harbor; the canal was still; they weren't calling for even a breath of wind. Then we got down by Eldred Rock and she started coming on northerly; at least we were running with it. Then a little later they came on the radio with a 'emergency gale warning.' Well, we were committed then, we couldn't do anything but keep on going. But right away, I went out on deck with a bunch of ten-penny nails and I nailed my hatch covers on. Good thing too, 'cause once she came on hard, sometimes I'd look outside and it seemed like the pilothouse was the only thing sticking up out of the water on the whole boat. If I hadn't nailed those hatch covers on, no way would we have made it."

—A friend

Even the largest vessels are no match for the big Lynn when the weather turns bad. Only a smooth, worn place on the rocks of Vanderbilt Reef and the graves of the unidentified dead in the Juneau cemetery are left from a terrible October night in 1918 when the liner *Princess Sophia* of the Canadian Pacific Railway fleet was lost. The *Sophia* left Skagway on the twenty-third of October with almost a full load: 343 passengers and crew. Many were coming out of the Klondike country for the winter. Eighty-seven were the officers and crew of ten steamboats from the Yukon River, their season done, the river frozen. Some were miners, coming out, headed "down below" with their stash after a season in the gold fields.

If there was a salon on board, and if they sold drinks, it would have been full.

Sometime around midnight the *Sophia* passed the lighthouse at Eldred Rock and disappeared down Lynn Canal in the thickening snow. Two hours later, perhaps unable to pick up the unlit buoy in the snow and black, she drove up on Vanderbilt Reef, in the middle of lower Lynn Canal, three miles from the nearest land.

It wasn't much of a night for a rescue. The *Anita Phillips*, a smaller vessel, had tried to anchor near the *Sophia* without success; she broke two pilothouse windows on her way to shelter at Tee Harbor, twelve

In one of the greatest tragedies ever to occur along the Inside Passage, the **Princess Sophia** *went ashore in 1918 on Vanderbilt Reef in Lynn Canal. All 343 passengers perished.*

miles south. Another one of the vessels standing by to render aid was the *King and Winge*, which had participated in the rescue of a group of sealers stranded in the Arctic a few years earlier. It was the *King and Winge* we tied our steel crab boat to when we arrived in Dutch Harbor in the wintry Aleutian Islands in 1971. She was then sixty-two years old, a lean, graceful wooden craft, working every day in one of the toughest fisheries in the world.

"They could have gotten off, that was the worst of it. It was blowin', yah sure, and the big boats couldn't get close to her, because of the reef, but they could have lowered their boats, and my dad and the other boats standing by could have saved them all. My dad said the way she was sitting on the reef, they could have lowered all the boats easy. That morning, they could have gotten them all off. But then by noon or so, she was coming on pretty good, northwest, with lots of snow, so Dad had to duck up into Tee Harbor, they couldn't stand it out there any longer, and whatever chance they had was gone."

—A friend

Ironically, one of the first ships to answer the *Sophia's* distress call was the lighthouse tender, *Cedar*, which was carrying a new lighted buoy to put at Vanderbilt Reef as soon as there was a break in the weather.

At dawn, half a dozen smaller vessels were standing by in the choppy waters. The *Sophia* was sitting upright on the reef, her bow almost totally high and dry, in no apparent danger. Though a sea was running, eyewitnesses stated that the *Sophia* could have launched her boats and transferred the passengers to the waiting vessels. However, another CPR ship, the *Princess Alice,* was arriving the next afternoon, and it was decided to await her arrival before transferring the people. Eight years earlier, the CPR steamer, *Princess May,* had grounded on Sentinel Island, three miles south, and had been refloated with little damage and no loss of life. Probably this experience was instrumental in the decision to leave the passengers aboard the *Sophia.* In any case, by early afternoon the snow and the wind had started up again, and the would-be rescuers sought shelter in Tee Harbor. The makings of the Northwest coast's greatest human tragedy were in place.

No one was on hand to see the *Sophia's* end that wild and snowy night. The wind blew down the canal harder and harder, until even those aboard the anchored rescue vessels in the shelter of Tee Harbor became concerned about dragging anchor. In the open wind tunnel that was the canal, the storm struck the high exposed side of the *Sophia* on the stern quarter, the shriek of the wind drowning out the sound of the steel plates ripping as the force of the gale twisted and finally pushed the *Sophia* off the reef. There was only that horrifying radio message, "For God's sake, come! We are sinking."

When the rescue vessels arrived at Vanderbilt Reef in the morning, the wind had dropped, but it was too late; only the masts of the *Sophia* were showing above water. Of her company, only a half-crazed dog was picked alive from the cold water; all 343 persons had perished.

When the sun shines, upper Lynn Canal is a spectacular place. Glaciers hang in the mountains. Sometimes when the air is still, one can hear clearly the thunder as pieces of ice the size of cottages break free to tumble and crash into the trees below.

For fishermen, it is the last hurrah. The last big salmon run of the season comes to a dramatic fjord called Chilkat Inlet. In a good year a person might double his season in this narrow spot, barely a mile and half by four. In a bad season, it might be his only chance.

And a chance it is. Four hundred-plus boats crowd in here, each with a net a quarter of a mile long. The nets are shallow and the fish mill beneath, waiting to enter the nearby river and swim to their spawning grounds. The milling fish rise, filling one net and leaving a neighbor with nothing. A big 'set' might be worth ten thousand dollars. Tempers run high.

"I *thought* I gave the guy plenty of room when I set out my net [in front of him]. But I guess he didn't think so. He steamed right over to us and stopped alongside. He had a gun stuck in his belt. It was a .45, I think. He pulled it out and pointed it at me. 'Pick up the net, pal,' he said, 'or you're dead meat. It's your choice . . .' My wife started screaming. I picked up my net. Hey, he was such a *mean*-looking dude, I would have picked it up even if he *hadn't* had a gun."

—A friend

Storms sweep up or down the canal in late September, right at the peak of the big fall run of dog salmon. Fishermen are faced with the dilemma of big fishing versus bad weather. If you've had a poor season, and all of a sudden you're getting two or three hundred dog salmon at ten dollars each every time you set your net, it's pretty hard to stop just because the wind blows.

"Three years I worked with him and we never had fishing like that. But it was a terrible night, black, blowing maybe fifty, running against the tide. But Dave, all he could see was them fish coming over the roller at ten bucks a pop. We filled up the fish hold and the fish boxes, and we were getting *really* low in the water, and still the fish were coming in, it seemed like every time Dave stepped on the pedal another dozen come over the roller. I kept thinking he'd say we'd have to stop, but we just kept picking them fish, and we kept gittin' lower and lower and finally I had to say something.

"'Say, Dave,' I shouted over the wind, 'maybe we got enough on now . . . maybe we should just call it good, or tow the net over to the tender . . .'

"He looked around suddenly at me, then he held up the fish he'd just picked, a big ten- or twelve-pounder. 'Got enough?' he asked me, shaking the fish all at the same time. 'You know how much these puppies are worth? Ten bucks a whack, and you want to go in? Hey, a thousand bucks goes pretty far in February.' Then he looked around, like he was jes' seeing the storm for the first time. 'Ah, we'll be all right, babes . . . this is just like some kind of Errol Flynn movie . . . there's the tenders right over there.' He nodded over to where you could see the lights of the tenders, laying in around behind the point. Some of the smarter fellas were already unloading. About five minutes after that we took a big one over the stern, the cockpit filled up, and the boat sank. We weren't in the water but a few minutes before one of the other boats picked us up, and we drug the boat ashore a couple of days later to dry it out and try to put the pieces back together. I didn't know which was worse—pitching fifteen thousand bucks of bad fish over the side or seeing the boat all busted up like that . . . son of a bitch should have gone in when I ast him to."

—A friend

Vancouver was just thirty-eight years old when he arrived off Cape Spencer in July of 1794. But already his health was showing signs of the constant strain of the voyage. He spent little time in the boats that last summer, leaving that work to his lieutenants and men. At the end of the month, with the exploration of the northern part of Southeast Alaska completed, the two ships sailed south to Port Conclusion in lower Chatham Strait. There, the small boats set out one last time to fill in the remaining blank spaces on the chart.

Two weeks later the boats were overdue and Vancouver was anxious. Finally, on the nineteenth of August in the middle of a rain squall, the boats hove into sight, the survey complete.

With grog for all hands and cheers ringing from one ship to another in a cove halfway around the world from England, there ended perhaps the most remarkable feat of navigation and exploration in modern times. In three summers exploring and charting an almost totally unknown coast, through persistent fogs, swift currents, and occasionally thick ice, with the loss of just one man from eating bad shellfish,

Vancouver had made a chart that varies in only minor ways from the best available today.

He came seeking to dispel the notion of a sea passage from west to east; he left a remarkable legacy in the form of his journals and charts.

THE GOLD RUSH. The Inside Passage ends in the muddy shallows at the mouth of the Taiya River, a mile or two north of Skagway, Alaska, and 962 miles from Seattle. Along the beach are what's left of lines of piling. Among the alder, spruce, and cedar on shore sit the remains of a long-dead town, Dyea.

For myself and the hundreds of fishermen who end up in upper Lynn Canal in late September, it is the end of the season as well. It is time to face the thousand-mile trip back to Puget Sound and our winter lives.

By then the weather has turned. The North Pacific storm systems have begun their regular fall track in from the ocean and up the coast. Lynn Canal, Stephens Passage, Clarence Strait. Dixon Entrance, Chatham Sound, Milbanke Sound—almost every major channel between Skagway and Seattle is oriented north and south, open to the fall storms. A day of traveling weather might only come after two or three of waiting. Each night comes earlier, each morning later. A boat and crew that hauled their last fish during the last week of September might not see their home port before Halloween.

For those who sailed north from Seattle in the frail iron and wooden ships in 1897 and 1898, excited by the prospect of gold after Tom Libby walked off the *Excelsior* with his suitcase carrying fifty thousand dollars in gold dust, Skagway and Dyea marked just the beginning.

For many who arrived in the first wave, there were no docks for their ships to tie to. They unloaded their stuff into small shallow lighters and then onto the beach. It was a long way to the high-tide line. Many were not acquainted with the sea and especially not the large tides in that part of Alaska. They tied goats and horses to whatever they could find on the flats—piling or rocks—while they took the first load to high ground and came back after a trip or two to find their gear under water, the animals they had transported a thousand miles drowned.

It was a real cold night. We walked along in the snow and we come to a fellow setting on the back of a Yukon sled. Yep, he was setting there in the middle of the road talking to hisself. His head was down on his hands. He looked plumb played out. He never seen us; he just went on talking to hisself. Over and over he'd say: "It's hell. Yes; multiply it by ten, and then multiply that by ten, and that ain't half as bad as this is. Yes, it's hell . . ." Them days it was every man for hisself. The faster a boat could unload and get out of there, the sooner it could get back to Seattle or Vancouver and pick up another load of suckers. A man shipped his outfit at his own risk. If he didn't get his stuff off the beach before the next tide, it was just his hard luck. No one else done no worrying about it.

—Mckeown, *The Trail Led North*

Yet still they came from almost every corner of the world, some arriving in the middle of winter, utterly unprepared for what awaited them. Most of the good ground had been already found, staked, and claimed before news of the strike ever hit Seattle. Of the thousands of people who left Seattle in the summer and fall of '97 and spring of '98, perhaps only a quarter actually staked a claim; perhaps fewer than a hundred found wealth in the quantities they had dreamed of. Yet when they arrived at the head of Lynn Canal on the ships, whatever tragedy, adventure, or success they were to have was still ahead of them. They stepped off buoyant, excited.

After their gear was ashore, Dawson City still lay more than three hundred miles away over extremely rugged country.

For many, that journey meant packing 1,500 pounds of supplies to the top of White Pass or Chilkoot Pass. The Canadian North West Mounted Police refused to let any enter the territory without a year's supplies, no doubt saving many lives with this rule. Those who had money could haul their outfit to the top of the pass on a cable tramway. Those without money packed it up, one load at a time up the steep trail, where a line of steps had been hacked into the snow and ice. If you stepped out of the line to take a breather, it sometimes took a while to get back in, so thick was the press of humanity trying to get to the diggings.

At Lake Bennett, the Klondike-bound crowd camped on the

shores, cut down the trees, sawed them into lumber, and fashioned crude boats. When the ice broke up in the lake, they pushed off from shore, headed for whatever fortune had in store for them.

> Every kind of boat was made in there. Several had made theirs square on each end. One was shaped just like a coffin, and not much bigger. Some leaked; some didn't steer. They had lots of things wrong with them. But a lot of the boats, made of whipsawed lumber, had beautiful lines and sailed as pretty as anything I ever did see on the Columbia. Yes, sir, that was an expedition, that fleet of boats getting ready to set out from Lake Bennett, come spring of '98.
>
> —Mckeown, *The Trail Led North*

One party of three in the fall of '98 set out in a crude boat down the Yukon from Dawson City in hopes of finding undiscovered gold-bearing streams. By the time they realized they were on a wild goose chase, they were too far downstream to pole their boat back up against the current. They were low on supplies, hadn't come across any settlements, and finally decided their only hope to survive the winter was to continue downriver and try to make it to the town of Saint Michael, over twelve hundred miles away. Each day it got colder; each night the river froze a little farther out toward the middle. They began paddling day and night, trying to make it out before the winter freeze trapped them. They ran out of food and had begun to chew on the leather of their shoes, when they saw a light downriver. They used their last matches, lit and held up the last of their firewood, until the steamer pulled up alongside their raft. It was a revenue cutter, the last boat to leave the Yukon that season. They were saved.

SKAGWAY. In October 1972 we lay in Skagway at the very end of our salmon season. We took the train up over White Pass and had lunch at the Lake Bennett Station. On the walls of the lunchroom were pictures from the past: gaunt faces from '97 and '98, bent-over men with frost-bitten hands, stumbling up over Chilkoot Pass with heavy packs. Men standing, taking a break for a moment from the backbreaking work in the saw pits, getting out the boards with which to build their boats. The faces that looked so hopeful lined up on the wharf at Seattle to board the steamers had taken on a somber, strained cast.

When the train rattled down from the pass to the sea in the afternoon, a raw, cold wind had come up. We stayed uptown to eat. The brief summer tourist season had come and gone, most of the buildings were dark, and the wind whirled dust and leaves around us in the empty streets. On the walls of the restaurant were more of those same serious, gold-hungry faces. As we walked back to the boat, it grew dark and cold, and we leaned into the wind to make headway. We got to the boat, fired up the oil stove, and snuggled into our bunks.

Deep in the night I awoke. The wind had come on stronger, heeling the boat over against the float and driving sleet against the windows. I drew on my oilskins and boots and went out into the windy black to double up our dock lines. The tide was high; every now and again a big sea would drive into the breakwater, and the spray carried to where we lay. The sleet turned to snow, driving horizontally downwind.

Six or eight salmon boats were in the harbor, straining against their lines, chafing against their fenders. In the dim light on the dock, I could see other oilskin-clad figures like myself, bent over, struggling with dock lines and fenders, their faces strained.

Finally, all was secure and I could go inside, shed the oilskins and get a cup of tea, and cozy up to the oil stove before going back to bed. I looked out at the night. The wind was blowing harder. A few figures still struggled against the wind and the snow, and I remembered what had so struck me out there.

The faces, seen in thin light on the windy dock, reminded me of those I'd seen earlier in pictures on the walls at the Lake Bennett Station and at Skagway—young, but lined already with the cares of the North.

Our lives so different, yet so much the same.

Acknowledgments

In a book such as this, which relies as much on recollection as research, I've sometimes had to try to piece together conversations or stories from years past, with few or no notes. I hope I've gotten them right, and apologize to the tellers for any mistakes. In particular, I want to thank the following people for their help along the way.

To Steve Trutich, for getting me started on this journey, in Iquique, Chile, in 1965.

To Lloyd Whaley, for picking me off the docks of Seattle and taking me to Alaska with him.

To George and Russell Fulton, for sharing so much of their knowledge with me, during a windy season in the Bering Sea in 1971.

To Bob and Jonni Dolan, for good stories and good companionship during many seasons in Southeast Alaska.

To Bob and Ann Holmstrand of the tender *Frigidland,* for sharing many decades of work in the North.

To John Enge, cannery superintendant, for taking on a green tenderman in the old ferrocement *Northwind.*

To Leonard Leach, for showing us the ropes on the "Garnet Point Run."

To Laland Daniels, tenderman and raconteur extraordinaire, for so much help over the years.

To John Pappenheimer, of *Alaska Fishermen's Journal,* for allowing me kind access to his files and recollections.

To my editor Ed Reading, for his patience.

To Marlene Blessing at Alaska Northwest Books, for her persistence in moving this project along.

To book designer Cameron Mason for doing such a fine job.

To those people, up and down the coast, who took the time to share so many stories with me.

And most of all, to my wife Mary Lou, for her patience and encouragement in a long project.

Bibliography

Blanchet, M. Wylie. *The Curve of Time*. Vancouver, B.C.: Whitecap Books, Ltd., 1990.

Canadian Hydrographic Service. *Sailing Directions, British Columbia Coast: (South Portion), Volume 1. (North Portion), Volume 2*. Sidney, B.C.: Department of Fisheries and Oceans, Institute of Ocean Sciences, 1965-1990.

Columbia Coast Missionary Society. *The Log*. 1907.

Hill, Beth. *Upcoast Summers*. Ganges, B.C.: Horsdal and Schubart, 1985.

Hydrographer of the [British] Navy. *British Columbia Pilot*, two volumes; revised by periodic supplements. Taunton, Somerset: Hydrographic Department, Ministry of Defence, Crown copyright Volume I 1979, Volume II 1976.

Mckeown, Martha Ferguson. *The Trail Led North: Mont Hawthorne's Story*. Portland, Ore.: Binford & Mort, 1960.

Morris, Frank, and W. R. Heath. *Marine Atlas of the Northwest*. Seattle: Bayless Enterprises, Inc., 1990.

Muir, John. *Travels in Alaska*. Boston: Houghton Mifflin Company, 1915.

Newell, Gordon R., editor. *The H. W. McCurdy Marine History of the Pacific Northwest*. Seattle: Superior Publishing Company, 1966.

Oman, Alan. "The Day They Took Our Town Away," in *Raincoast Chronicles: Forgotten Villages of the BC Coast*. Madeira Park, B.C.: Harbor Publishing, 1987.

Upton, Joe. *Alaska Blues: A Fisherman's Journal*. Anchorage: Alaska Northwest Books, 1977.

Vancouver, George. *A Voyage of Discovery to the North Pacific Ocean and Around the World*. London: 1798.

White, Howard, editor. *Raincoast Chronicles: Forgotten Villages of the BC Coast*. Madeira Park, B.C.: Harbor Publishing, 1987.

Index

Note: Boldface type indicates a photo and/or text in a photo caption.

More Explorations of Northern Waters . . .

Ray Troll's Shocking Fish Tales: *Fish, Romance, and Death in Pictures,*
Illustrations by Ray Troll, Text by Brad Matsen.
"This book is for fishing aficionados who can't get fish out of their heads . . ."
—*Alaska Fisherman's Journal.* Ketchikan artist Ray Troll, known for his "truth stranger than fishin'" T-shirt images, partners up with writer Brad Matsen to tell tales of fish and fisher folk, halibut too powerful to be eaten, the romantic ways of fish, sport fishing fish-outs, scary fish, and more. 67 color illustrations, 8 black-and-white illustrations
104 pages, softbound, $15.95   ISBN 0-88240-416-4

Where the Sea Breaks Its Back: *The Epic Story of Early Naturalist Georg W. Steller and the Russian Exploration of Alaska,* by Corey Ford.
Illustrated by Lois Darling.
This is the dramatic story of naturalist Georg W. Steller, who sailed with Vitus Bering in 1742, and whose legacy to nature lovers today includes discoveries such as the Steller's jay and the Steller's sea lion, as well as an awareness of the possibility of a species' extinction at the hands of humans.
224 pages, softbound, $12.95   ISBN 0-88240-394-X

The Hidden Coast: *Kayak Explorations from Alaska to Mexico,*
by Joel W. Rogers.
"I greatly enjoyed Joel Rogers's book for its sense of adventure and its wonderful pictures."—Paul Theroux, author of *The Mosquito Coast.* Visit the wet, sunny world of the Pacific Coast, from Alaska's Prince William Sound to Mexico's La Manzanilla with sea kayaker and photographer Joel Rogers. Readers will experience the wildlife, wilderness beauty, and unique anthropological features of seldom-seen, rugged coastal locales. 72 color photographs; 17 maps
168 pages, softbound, $19.95   ISBN 0-88240-403-2

Baidarka: *The Kayak,* by George Dyson.
"A grand, detailed book that will be the standard for years to come."—James A. Michener. George Dyson's book begins with the coming of the Russians to Alaska and their discovery of the Aleuts' skill with kayaks (*baidarkas*). It continues with Dyson's rediscovery of the baidarka and his far-ranging travels with his boats. 93 color photographs, 32 black-and-white photographs; 4 watercolors; 56 drawings
231 pages, softbound, $19.95   ISBN 0-88240-315-X

Ask for these books at your favorite bookstore, or contact
Alaska Northwest Books™ for a complete catalog.

Alaska Northwest Books™
A division of GTE Discovery Publications, Inc.
P.O. Box 3007, Bothell, WA 98041-3007
1-800-343-4567

About the Author

JOE UPTON is a writer and fisherman, with fifteen years experience exploring the waters of Alaska and British Columbia. He currently lives in Bainbridge Island, Washington, with his wife and two children.